The God Who Hears

The God Who Hears

HOW THE STORY OF THE BIBLE SHAPES OUR PRAYERS

Sarah Ivill

Reformation Heritage Books
Grand Rapids, Michigan

The God Who Hears
© 2022 by Sarah Ivill

All rights reserved. No part of this book may be used or reproduced in any manner whatsoever without written permission except in the case of brief quotations embodied in critical articles and reviews. Direct your requests to the publisher at the following addresses:

Reformation Heritage Books
3070 29th St. SE
Grand Rapids, MI 49512
616-977-0889
orders@heritagebooks.org
www.heritagebooks.org

Unless otherwise indicated, Scripture taken from the New King James Version®. Copyright © 1982 by Thomas Nelson. Used by permission. All rights reserved.

Scripture quotations marked ESV are from The ESV® Bible (The Holy Bible, English Standard Version®), copyright © 2001 by Crossway, a publishing ministry of Good News Publishers. Used by permission. All rights reserved.

All italics in Scripture quotations have been added by the author.

Printed in the United States of America
22 23 24 25 26 27/10 9 8 7 6 5 4 3 2 1

Library of Congress Cataloging-in-Publication Data

Names: Ivill, Sarah, author.
Title: The God who hears : how the story of the Bible shapes our prayers /
  Sarah Ivill.
Description: Grand Rapids, MI : Reformation Heritage Books, [2022] |
  Includes index.
Identifiers: LCCN 2021049488 (print) | LCCN 2021049489 (ebook) |
  ISBN 9781601789167 (paperback) | ISBN 9781601789174 (epub)
Subjects: LCSH: Prayer—Biblical teaching—Textbooks. | Bible—Theology—Text-
  books. | BISAC: RELIGION / Prayer | RELIGION / Biblical Studies / General
Classification: LCC BS680.P64 I95 2022 (print) | LCC BS680.P64 (ebook) | DDC
  248.3/2—dc23/eng/20211118
LC record available at https://lccn.loc.gov/2021049488
LC ebook record available at https://lccn.loc.gov/2021049489

For additional Reformed literature, request a free book list from Reformation Heritage Books at the above regular or email address.

To my beloved Savior, my Great High Priest,
Who has passed through the heavens,
Jesus the Son of God,
Who is able to sympathize with my weaknesses
And who in all points was tempted as I am,
Yet without sin,
And who has given me the gift to boldly
Come to the throne of grace,
That I may obtain mercy and
Find grace to help in time of need.

—based on Hebrews 4:14–16

Contents

A Note from Sarah

This book is a biblical theology of prayer. Understanding prayer as it unfolds from Genesis through Revelation reveals the foundation and motivation for prayer. We begin with the truth that God has initiated a conversation with us. He has created us to be in relationship with Him. We don't have to wonder if "someone up there" hears our pleas; we can be confident our Creator hears us, knows us, and loves us. Studying prayer through the unfolding story of Scripture will teach us how to pray, but more importantly it will reveal the covenant God to whom we pray. His ears are open, and He will hear His daughters. He delights in our prayers and praise. In prayer we come before the Lord of all the earth, the Creator of our body and soul, the Savior of the world. My prayer for you as you study the story of Scripture is simple. I want you, dear reader, to delight in prayer—and not just in prayer but also in the God who invites us to pray.

Acknowledgments

I was introduced to biblical theology through Westminster Theological Seminary when many years ago I read the required books for their master of divinity degree program. Authors like Geerhardus Vos, Herman Ridderbos, Edmund Clowney, Dennis Johnson, Iain Duguid, and Greg Beale have been of tremendous benefit to me. So I was excited when Reformation Heritage Books, especially Jay Collier and David Woollin, was enthusiastic about and supportive of this writing project.

I also want to thank the pastors of Christ Covenant Church (PCA) for faithfully proclaiming the word of God each week and making prayer a central part of worship as well as everything else we do. I'm grateful also for the women in my Bible study class who allow me the privilege of coming alongside them in prayer and who faithfully pray for me.

Thank you to my dad and mom, David and Judy Gelaude, who have faithfully prayed for me over the years. I love you both more than words can express, and it's my delight to pray for both of you.

Thank you to my husband, Charles, who prays with me and for me often, especially for my writing projects, and who grants me the privilege of praying for him. And thank you to our children, Caleb, Hannah, Daniel, and Lydia: your prayers are precious as I watch you grow in the faith that your dad and I hold so dear.

Finally, thank you to my heavenly Father, to my Lord and Savior Jesus Christ, and to the Holy Spirit for making prayer possible. It is one of my greatest joys and privileges to pray to the Father through the Son by the Holy Spirit. And it is one of my greatest comforts that the Spirit helps me in my weakness because I don't know what to pray for as I ought, but the Spirit Himself intercedes for me according to the will of God (see Rom. 8:26–27).

Introduction to a
Biblical Theology of Prayer

I have always loved stories. When I was younger, one of my favorite things to do was sit with a good book and read. Now that I'm a mother, one of my favorite things is to sit with my four children and read. Oftentimes I get so lost in the story I'm reading that I lose track of time. I would rather not stop for lunch because I want to see how the story progresses or ends. In many cases the characters become our friends as we're swept up with the story and imagine ourselves there with them.

But there's one story that can't be beat. I fell in love with this story when I was a young girl, and by God's grace I have never found one I love better—the story of the Bible. From the Law to the Prophets to the Psalms to the Gospels to the Epistles to Revelation, I'm often moved to tears of conviction and comfort as I read God's story. The overarching narrative of the Bible that speaks of creation, the fall, redemption, and consummation fits perfectly together as one organic whole. We shouldn't be surprised at its cohesiveness. The divine author, the Holy Spirit, inspired each of the human authors. No human could write such a story. The story of the Bible is to be highly esteemed. Think of "the heavenliness of the matter, the efficacy of the doctrine, the majesty of the style, the consent of all the parts, the scope of the whole (which is to give all glory to God), the full discovery it makes of the only way of humankind's salvation, the many other incomparable excellencies, and the entire perfection thereof." Yet even so, only the Holy Spirit can work in our hearts so as to bring us to a "full persuasion and assurance of the infallible truth and divine authority thereof."[1]

Since there is no other book on our shelves that can rival this story, I want to whet your appetite for studying the Bible and, particularly in this book, the theme of prayer in the Bible. Once you understand the Bible for the story that it is, you will be transformed. Your studies will be different, as well as your approach to your career, marital status, ministry, parenting, or care for aging parents. You will begin to see your smaller story in light of the larger story of the Bible, and you will begin to understand things you never understood before. So what is this great story that no other author has been able to rival?

The Story Is Covenantal

The primary author of the story of Scripture is the covenant-making and covenant-keeping God, but He used human authors inspired by His Spirit to write sixty-six books of the Bible over hundreds of years. This story speaks of the history of redemption that begins with creation (Genesis 1–2) and the fall (Genesis 3) and ends with the consummation of God's kingdom (Revelation 21–22). The rest of the Bible focuses on redemption, so it's easy to see why Christ is the central character in the story.

The covenantal framework of Scripture reveals the covenant of redemption, the covenant of works, and the covenant of grace. The covenant of redemption is described in Ephesians 1:4, which teaches us that God the Father chose us in Christ "before the foundation of the world, that we should be holy and without blame before Him." The Father has appointed our redemption, the Son has accomplished it, and the Holy Spirit applies it.

---

1. *The Westminster Confession of Faith and Catechisms* (Lawrenceville, Ga.: Christian Education and Publications, 2007), 1.5. All subsequent quotations of the Westminster Confession of Faith (WCF) and the Larger (WLC) and Shorter Catechisms (WSC) are taken from this edition.

The covenant of works, described in Genesis 1–2, was initiated by God with Adam and involved keeping the Sabbath day holy, ruling and multiplying, marriage and procreation, and a command. The Lord God told Adam that he could eat of any tree in the garden except one, the tree of the knowledge of good and evil. If he ate of that tree, he would die. Tragically, Adam failed to obey, and all humankind fell with him in this first sin.

But death will not have the final word. The covenant of grace is established in Genesis 3:15. God promises that He will put enmity between the serpent and the woman, between the serpent's offspring and the woman's offspring. The woman's offspring would bruise the serpent's head, and the serpent would bruise His heel. This is the gospel in seed form. Ultimately, the woman's offspring is Christ. Christ defeated sin and death on the cross, triumphing over all His enemies. The Westminster Larger Catechism 31 states, "The covenant of grace was made with Christ as the second Adam, and in him with all the elect as his seed." This covenant of grace is progressively revealed throughout Scripture in God's covenant with Noah (Gen. 6:17–22; 8:20–22; 9:1–17), Abraham (Gen. 12:1–3; 15:1–21; 17:1–2), Moses (Exodus 19–24), David (2 Samuel 7), and in the new covenant (Jer. 31:31–34), all of which are fulfilled in Jesus Christ (2 Cor. 1:20).

The Story Is Historical

We cannot read passages of Scripture about prayer without an understanding of their historical context. Genesis 1–2 introduces us to the Creator and covenant King who created Adam and Eve, real historical people. The fall of Adam and Eve into sin isn't a legend, but a true, historical incident that had radical implications for all humankind. Romans 5:12 states, "Through one man sin entered the world, and death through sin, and thus death spread to all men, because all sinned." Cain's murder of Abel was a real historical event. Likewise, the stories of Noah and the ark, the Tower of Babel, and the dispersion of the nations are historical facts.

As we move from Genesis to Revelation, we are reading about real history, yet it is selective history. The stories of creation, the fall, the flood, and God's covenant with Noah and the patriarchs are important snapshots that are foundational to understanding the rest of the story. God's covenant with Moses, His covenant with David, and the glory days of Solomon give us a glimpse of the coming kingdom of Christ. The exiles of Israel at the hand of the Assyrians and Judah at the hand of the Babylonians reveal how sinful humankind is and how desperate is their need for a Savior. The return to the land under Ezra, Nehemiah, and Zerubbabel is a glimmer of hope, but still only a shadow of the glory to come in Christ.

The unfolding history of the Old Testament is concerned with the gospel. As Paul says in Galatians 3:8, "And the Scripture, foreseeing that God would justify the Gentiles by faith, preached the gospel to Abraham beforehand, saying, 'In you all the nations shall be blessed.'" The Old Testament Scriptures preach the gospel! As Iain Duguid says, "Centrally, the Old Testament is a book about Christ, and more specifically, about his sufferings and the glories that will follow—that is, it is a book about the promise of a coming Messiah through whose sufferings God will establish his glorious, eternal kingdom.... The central thrust of every passage leads us in some way to the central message of the gospel."[2] So as we study passages about prayer from the Bible, we can be certain that they will somehow lead us to the good news of Christ's life, death, and resurrection.

The unfolding history of the Old Testament continues in the New Testament. The Gospels begin with the inauguration of Christ's kingdom. Then the book of Acts, Paul's letters to the churches, and the General Epistles deal with the beginning of the Interadvent age. Finally, the apostle John describes the consummation of the kingdom at the end of the book of Revelation.

---

2. Iain M. Duguid, "Old Testament Hermeneutics," in *Seeing Christ in All of Scripture: Hermeneutics at Westminster Theological Seminary*, ed. Peter A. Lillback (Philadelphia, Pa.: Westminster Seminary Press, 2016), 17, 19.

The Story Is Redemptive

You barely begin reading the Bible when the breathtaking story of creation takes a turn for the worse. Adam and Eve failed to obey the Lord God and are forced to leave the garden of Eden, the place where they had enjoyed His presence. The Lord takes the initiative to redeem fallen humankind, but it's not an immediate transformation. The story is thousands of years long and is filled with anger and arrogance, lying and lust, malice and murder, sin and shame. The plot takes many surprising turns and has several alarming twists. On many occasions God's promises seem thwarted, and oftentimes His plans seem to hang in the balance. But through it all a ray of redemptive hope glimmers in the darkness.

Because the story is redemptive, the Redeemer is the key who holds the Old and New Testaments together. The promises of God, the prophecies spoken on behalf of the Lord, the sacrifices offered on the altars, the circumcision of every Jewish male, the Passover, and other feasts of Israel pointed forward to the Christ to come. These were sufficient and effective by God's Spirit to instruct and edify the elect in the promised Messiah, by whom they had forgiveness of sins and the gift of eternal life (WCF 7.5).

In the New Testament the gospel bursts forth in all its glory. Though it is not like the glory of Solomon's temple, which could be seen outwardly, it has a far superior glory. The true temple arrived, radiating "the glory as of the only begotten of the Father, full of grace and truth" (John 1:14). The sacrifices of the Old Testament were no longer needed. Christ, the final sacrifice, had fulfilled their purposes. The preaching of the word of God and the sacraments of baptism and the Lord's Supper proclaim the gospel to all nations superiorly (WCF 7.6).

The Story Is Christ-Centered

Jesus Himself tells us He is the central character of Scripture. In Luke 24 we learn of two disciples who were trying to put together the story of Jesus. They had been in Jerusalem and witnessed the events at the end of Jesus's life. Now they were on their way home to Emmaus, and they were deeply distressed. Their hope had been deflated. They thought Jesus was the one to redeem Israel, but instead He was crucified and buried. Indeed, the tomb was empty, but Jesus was nowhere to be seen.

Jesus says to them, "'O foolish ones, and slow of heart to believe in all that the prophets have spoken! Ought not the Christ to have suffered these things and to enter into His glory?' And beginning at Moses and all the Prophets, He expounded to them in all the Scriptures the things concerning Himself" (Luke 24:25–27).

It was the privilege of not only these two Emmaus disciples to hear Jesus tell His story but also of the disciples who had been with Him during His earthly ministry. Luke tells us later in the same chapter that Jesus opened their minds to understand the Scriptures, everything written about Him in the Law of Moses and the Prophets and the Psalms. These things had to be fulfilled, and Jesus was telling them that He was the fulfillment (Luke 24:44–47).

Jesus is the second Adam, who did not sin but was obedient to death on the cross. He is the Seed of the woman, who crushed the serpent's head (Gen. 3:15). He is the final Noah, who saved His people through the cross (Eph. 2:16). He is the final Abraham, in whom all the families of the earth are blessed (Acts 2:38–39; 3:25–26; Gal. 3:13–14, 29). He is the final Isaac, who was sacrificed for our sin. He is the final Passover Lamb (Ex. 12:13). He is the final sacrifice, whose blood atoned for our sins (Lev. 16:14–16). He is the final and perfect priest, who is greater than Aaron (Heb. 9:11–12). He is the true Israel, who was tested and tried in the wilderness and obeyed (Matt. 4:1–11). He is the one lifted up to deliver sinners from death (Num. 21:9). He is the Prophet greater than Moses (Deut. 18:15–22). He is the one who gives grace to covenant breakers (Deut. 27:1–26). He is the ark of the covenant and the blood on the mercy seat (Heb. 9:1–14). He is the true bread of life and the light of the world (John 6:48, 51; 8:12). He is the Commander of the army of the Lord (Josh. 5:14). He is the final Judge, who never fell into sin but delivered His people by taking their judgment for them (2 Cor. 5:21). He is the final kinsman-redeemer greater than Boaz (Ruth 3:12–13). He is the final psalmist, who leads His people in praise to God (Heb. 2:12). He is the final Davidic king, who reigns in perfect justice and righteousness (John 18:37). He is the final Solomon, who is not only full of wisdom but is wisdom Himself (1 Cor. 1:30). He is the final Prophet, who suffered for His people and did so without opening His mouth in retaliation (Isaiah 53). And He is the Great Shepherd of the sheep (Ezek. 34:11–24).

Why a Biblical Theology of Prayer?

During my years of teaching the Bible to women, I have presented the time line of Scripture. I keep before my students the big story of Scripture—creation, the fall, redemption, and consummation. In between these big events I teach smaller events that occur throughout the history of redemption. My aim is for women to dig into the Bible, reading it chronologically and studying texts in light of their original context as well as in light of the redemptive-historical context. If they are studying the New Testament I ask them to flip back to the Old Testament, and if they are studying the Old Testament I ask them to turn to the New Testament. I want them to see how the texts of Scripture are related, how they hold together as one cohesive whole, and how Christ is the interpretive key. My aim is no different in this book. I have devoted our study to one theme, prayer, and trace it throughout redemptive history in order to show its progressive revelation throughout Scripture and how it is organically related to the whole story, with Christ at the center.

The study of biblical theology is simply interested in the history of the unfolding of redemption.[3] The Bible is divided into different periods of redemption, such as creation, the fall, the flood, the call of Abram, the exodus from Egypt, and the coming of Christ. It focuses on the history and cohesion of Scripture with Christ at the center

---

3. Geerhardus Vos, *Biblical Theology: Old and New Testaments* (1975; repr., Edinburgh: Banner of Truth, 2007), 14.

of it all. As we think about the importance of a biblical theology of prayer, we should remember several important things.[4]

First, our study is in the church and for the church. As we study with other believers, we are all edified and encouraged. A biblical theology of prayer isn't an end in itself. Its aim is to glorify God and enjoy Him as we come to know Him better through His word. As we come to know Him more, we grow in loving Him and our neighbor by the power of His Spirit at work in us.

Second, we learn to read the Bible chronologically. There's a narrative storyline of Scripture interspersed with commentary on the storyline. If you want to read the narrative storyline of the Old Testament, you would read Genesis through Judges, Samuel through Kings, Daniel, Esther, Ezra through Nehemiah, and then Chronicles. If you want to follow the commentary on this narrative, after reading Kings and before starting Daniel, you would read Jeremiah, Ezekiel, Isaiah, the Minor Prophets, Ruth, Psalms, Job, Proverbs, Ecclesiastes, Song of Songs, and Lamentations.[5] If you want to read the narrative storyline of the New Testament, you would read the Gospels, Acts, and Revelation. If you want to follow the commentary on this narrative, after reading Acts and before reading Revelation, you would read Paul's epistles as well as the General Epistles.

Third, as we engage in a biblical theology of prayer, we become sensitive to the genres of Scripture and the biblical authors' intended meaning. We stop misunderstanding texts out of context and instead seek to understand what the author intended us to learn. This means we read poetry as poetry and wisdom books as wisdom books. We don't read apocalyptic literature, such as Daniel 7–10 and Revelation, as if we're reading the narrative of Numbers.

---

4. For a good definition of *biblical theology*, the one that informed my five points, see B. S. Rosner, "Biblical Theology," in *New Dictionary of Biblical Theology*, ed. T. Desmond Alexander, Brian S. Rosner, D. A. Carson, and Graeme Goldsworthy (Downers Grove, Ill.: IVP Academic, 2000), 10.

5. Stephen G. Dempster, *Dominion and Dynasty: A Theology of the Hebrew Bible*, New Studies in Biblical Theology (Downers Grove, Ill.: IVP Academic, 2003), 51.

Fourth, the overarching story is drilled into our minds as we study the theme of prayer in Scripture. This helps us have a biblical worldview in which to interpret all the events of our lives. This is our Father's world, which He created. On the one hand, we can affirm the goodness of the creation. On the other hand, evil, suffering, and sin are the result of the fall. But there's hope in the midst of this fallen world; the Redeemer, Jesus Christ, has come and inaugurated His kingdom and is coming again to consummate it.

Finally, our study of biblical theology exalts Jesus Christ. It is Christ-centered, meaning He is the hero of the story. "For all the promises of God in Him are Yes, and in Him Amen, to the glory of God through us" (2 Cor. 1:20).

* * * * *

Do you like a good story? Look no further than Scripture. Don't delay digging in to study the theme of prayer. As we trace this theme throughout redemptive history in order to show its progressive revelation throughout Scripture and how it is organically related to the whole story, with Christ at the center, by God's grace, the majesty of His word will move and purify you. The consent of all the parts will comfort you, the scope of the whole will strengthen you, and its light and power will convince you of your sin and need of a Savior (WLC 4).

The Lord Who Calls

From Creation to the Fall

One of my fondest memories about dating my husband is how he initiated our relationship. He was very purposeful in his words and communicated his intentions clearly. I didn't have to wonder if he liked me or wanted to date me—or even if he wanted to marry me. He told me. He called me and asked me out. He spoke about his fear of messing up our friendship in order to find out if marriage was right for us. When the time was right, he spoke those words I had longed to hear: "Will you marry me?" And on our wedding day, he spoke words of commitment to me.

In our relationships we like other people to take the initiative in displaying their affection for us or appreciation of us. I still remember the email from an author and series editor who had reviewed one of my Bible study books and thought I was the woman to write one of the books in her series. That email meant so much to me. She had initiated a working relationship with me after exploring my work and invited me to partner with her in communicating the gospel of Jesus Christ.

It's likely you have your own stories of people who have initiated relationships with you. I hope the first relationship that comes to your mind is the one that the Lord God initiated with you when He called you to be His child. Do you remember your first prayer? Maybe it was a simple, "Help, I know I'm a sinner in need of grace. I want you to be Lord and Savior of my life." Whatever the content of your prayer, you talked with God! You wouldn't have done that on your own. He had to give you the grace to call on the name of the Lord. In other words, He called to you so that you could call on Him.

I read a book to my children titled *That's When I Talk with God.* I love the simplicity of it. It teaches my children that they can talk to God all day long about anything and everything. Scripture teaches us that the reason we can talk to God all day long about anything and everything is because He talked to us first. He pursued us so that we can pray. How beautiful is that? If you're looking for a reason to pray, look no further. The Creator has called to His creation. He wants a relationship with us.

The Beginning of the Story

In Scripture, the greatest story of stories, there are probably not many words more familiar to us than, "In the beginning God created the heavens and the earth" (Gen. 1:1). In the first chapter of Genesis, as well as at the beginning of chapter 2, is the glorious account of God creating the heavens and the earth. It's a bit like an overview of a very important subject—an outline, if you will. But one part of the outline is so important that in chapter 2 God gives us more details. Just as we think the curtain is closing on the creation account, we read again about the creation of man and woman (vv. 7–25).

We already learned from Genesis 1 that the three persons of the Godhead "created man in His own image; in the image of God He created him" (Gen. 1:27). We also learned that "male and female He created them," and He blessed them and commissioned them (vv. 27–28). But in chapter 2 we read more details about God's creation of humankind: "And the LORD God formed man of the dust of the ground, and breathed into his nostrils the breath of life" (2:7). Then, God put him in a place that He planted. This garden in Eden was filled with trees that the Lord God made to spring up out of the ground. They were pleasant to look at, and they produced delicious food. Two trees stood in the middle, the tree of life and the tree of the knowledge of good and evil. As Adam walked through the garden, not only would he have seen pleasant sights but also he would have heard pleasant sounds. There was a built-in watering system, a river that flowed out of Eden and divided into four rivers.

In this place God purposed for Adam to work the garden and keep it. Such work would make any man hungry, and the Lord provided good food for Adam. The man could eat from every tree in the garden except one: "But of the tree of the knowledge of good and evil you shall not eat, for in the day that you eat of it you shall surely die" (Gen. 2:17). This was more than sufficient, an abundance of food. No one could ever go hungry with such a steady supply of nourishment. There would never be a reason to eat of the forbidden tree because the man had plenty of luscious fruit from which to choose. Furthermore, eating fruit from the forbidden tree was deadly.

A Voluntary Relationship

How kind it was of the Lord to come to Adam in the garden and speak with him. He was not a Creator who left His creature alone to fend for himself. Instead, He voluntarily initiated a relationship with humankind by way of covenant. God wanted to speak with His creation. More amazingly, He desired His creation to speak with Him. The first covenant God made with Adam was the covenant of works. He gave Adam a command not to eat from the tree of the knowledge of good and evil. If Adam obeyed he would receive life, but if he disobeyed he would die. Adam was in a special position as the head of the human race. His choice affected all humankind. It sounds easy, right? Adam was in a pleasant place with fabulous food and serene sounds. His work was wonderful and his communion with the Creator perfect.

But something wasn't good. The Lord didn't like that Adam was alone. And after God gave him the task of naming all the animals, Adam probably realized he didn't like being alone. No animal that he named was like him. None of them walked or talked as he did. But when God put him into a deep sleep and made Eve out of his rib and brought her to Adam, he knew that she was like him. "*This is now* bone of my bones and flesh of my flesh" (Gen. 2:23) he declared, as though he had been eagerly searching for a companion and, as he named animal after animal, had become increasingly aware that one wasn't to be found. But God gave Eve to Adam at just the right time. And the two became the happiest married couple who have ever walked this earth. Their communion with their Creator and with each other was perfectly blessed. The Lord God talked with them and they talked with Him in the glorious garden.

A Breach in the Relationship

But one day something terrible happened. Someone other than God started talking to Adam and Eve. Satan, who had rebelled against God and become His archenemy, crafted deceptive words to speak to Eve. He questioned God's trustworthiness and goodness in order to get Eve (and Adam, who was with her) to question His trustworthiness and goodness. "Has God indeed said, 'You shall not eat of every tree of the garden'?" (Gen. 3:1). Satan tempted them with words to partake of that which was forbidden to them: "You will not surely die. For God knows that in the day you eat of it your eyes will be opened, and you will be like God, knowing good and evil" (vv. 4–5). And instead of turning and talking with God, they turned and talked with the serpent. This decision cost them dearly. Adam and Eve fell into sin, and all humankind with them.

Their eyes experienced the effects of sin first: "Then the eyes of both of them were opened, and they knew that they were naked; and they sewed fig leaves together and made themselves coverings" (Gen. 3:7). But then their ears experienced the effects of their sin—and how terrible it must have been! The sound of the Lord God walking in the garden in the cool of the day, signaling them to come walk and talk with Him—a sound they used to love and anticipate—was now dreadful. Instead of wanting to hear His voice, they hid because they had listened to Satan's voice. "And they heard the sound of the LORD God walking in the garden…[and they] hid themselves from the presence of the LORD God among the trees of the garden" (v. 8).

The Garden Courtroom

Surely the Lord God could have killed Adam and Eve on the spot, having never spoken another word to them. He certainly would have been right and just in doing so. But instead, the Lord called to Adam and Eve. They never would have called to Him. They were spiritually dead in their sin. They hid from the presence of the Lord. If the Creator was ever going to talk with His creation again, He would have to do the initiating. And amazingly, He did.

When the Lord God did speak to them, it wasn't the sound of a father calling to his children to climb on his lap to hear a story. It was the sound of a father who calls his children into the house to find out who has broken his belongings because they disobeyed his rules. It was the scene of a courtroom. The Lord God's question "Where are you?" (Gen. 3:9) wasn't an invitation to enjoy a nice walk and talk with Him, but an exhortation to stand before the Judge, tell the truth, and plead guilty.

The Lord God addressed Adam first, the one with whom He had made the covenant of works. Adam was the head of his wife as well as of the whole human race. In a series of questions, the Lord God led Adam and Eve in confession of sin: "Who told you that you were naked? Have you eaten from the tree of which I commanded you that you should not eat? …What is this you have done?" (Gen. 3:11, 13). It wasn't a model confession, to be sure. Adam blamed Eve: "The woman whom You gave to be with me, she gave me of the tree, and I ate" (v. 12). And Eve blamed the serpent, "The serpent deceived me, and I ate" (v. 13). But even so, they admitted that they had disobeyed God. In this we see God's grace at work in the first two sinners' hearts. Sinners don't confess their sin naturally. They hide. But when the Lord God calls to His people, He gives them grace to see their sin, hate it, and forsake it.

Have you, dear reader, ever come before the Lord God and confessed your sin? Have you pleaded guilty? Have you asked Him to be your Lord and Savior? You don't have to hide because of your sin. The safest place to go when we sin is to the Savior. He pleads on our behalf so that we will not be guilty anymore. Do you have loved ones, neighbors, or friends ensnared in sin? Why not stop right now and make 2 Timothy 2:25–26 a prayer: *Father, please "grant them repentance, so that they may know the truth, and that they may come to their senses and escape the snare of the devil," who has taken them "captive…to do his will."*

Good News in the Garden

How terrible it must have been for Adam and Eve to hear God speak the word "cursed" to the serpent (Gen. 3:14) and then to hear the consequences they would each face for their sin (vv. 16–19). And yet how hope must have filled their hearts when they heard Him say to the serpent,

> And I will put enmity
> Between you and the woman,
> And between your seed and her Seed;
> He shall bruise your head,
> And you shall bruise His heel. (v. 15)

This is the first statement of the gospel in the Bible. The covenant of works was not the final and decisive covenant. As the Westminster Larger Catechism 31 says, "The covenant of grace was made with Christ as the second Adam, and in him with all the elect as his seed." Genesis 3:15 is an example of one of the promises by which the covenant of grace was administered under the Old Testament (WLC 34). It was also administered by prophecies, sacrifices, circumcision, the Passover, and other types and ordinances, which all foreshadowed Christ and were sufficient for that time in redemptive history to build up the elect in faith in the promised Messiah, by whom they had forgiveness of sins and eternal life. Once Christ came, this same covenant of grace was and continues to be administered through the preaching of God's word and the administration of the sacraments of baptism and the Lord's Supper (WLC 35).

The Final Word

God always has the final word. Eve shouldn't have listened to the serpent, and Adam shouldn't have listened to Eve. They should have listened to God. When God had every right never to speak with them again, He instead spoke a word of grace. He would ensure that there would still be communion between the Creator and His creatures. He would make sure that His people would still be able to talk with Him. Yes, He had to drive them out of the garden. Yes, it would be a road of discomfort, disunity, difficulty, and death. But God would still speak with His people. The Seed of the woman would crush the head of the serpent. The sinless One would sympathize with and save sinners. The suffering One would extend mercy and grace in time of need (Heb. 4:14–16). The Lord God would not stop calling to His people. And His people would begin to learn what it means to call on the name of the Lord.

* * * * *

When was the last time someone pursued you in a relationship because he or she valued you? No matter how great it made you feel, it pales in comparison to the significance of the Creator calling to you, voluntarily initiating a relationship with you, longing to talk with you. He doesn't leave us wondering if He likes us. We know He does. He has initiated a relationship with His people and secures it with the blood of His own Son, Jesus Christ. Won't you respond to Him by speaking with Him? Tell Him that you stand in awe of His character. Tell Him about the unkind word you spoke to your spouse, the test you cheated on, the ugly look you gave your child, the envy that filled your heart, the anger that welled up inside you, the lustful look you took at the screen or the neighbor, or the worship you gave to an object instead of to Him. Thank Him for the people He has put in your life, the places He has appointed you to serve, and the possessions He has given you. Talk to Him about the need you, your loved ones, friends, and neighbors have, asking Him to save the prodigal child, heal the cancerous body, restore a broken marriage, deliver a friend from an alcohol addiction, and empower a missionary to proclaim the gospel clearly to a different people group. Don't hide in your sin and shame. Don't think He doesn't see you. He calls you by name. Run to Him and talk with Him. He is the Lord who calls and who cares.

Time to Ponder and Pray

1. Describe a time someone took the initiative in a relationship in order to display his or her affection for you or appreciation of you. How did it make you feel? How does it make you feel that the Lord initiates a relationship with you in which you can pray to Him?

2. How do you teach your children or the children in your church to pray? What would you say if someone asked you, "Why should I pray?" *by example*

3. What did you learn in the beginning of the story of Scripture that was new to you or that reminded you of something you had forgotten?

4. God voluntarily initiates a relationship with His people. Why does this motivate you to pray? How can you incorporate prayer into your daily life? How can you set aside a regular time to pray with your spouse, children, or a friend?

5. How has sin put a breach in the relationship between God and humankind? What has God done to bridge the breach?

6. Why does the good news that came in the garden (Gen. 3:15) comfort you? How could you use this verse to share the gospel with a friend? *His GRACE - Battle is already won - Christ is Coming -*

7. How does it affect you to know that God is present with you in your discomfort, disunity, or difficulty and that He is ready for you to speak with Him? *Hope - Comfort Peace*

8. Since God speaks to His people through His word, the Bible, why is it important to base your prayers on Scripture? *NOT alone in struggles -*

9. In light of what you've learned in this chapter, write out a prayer to God.

10. Seek to memorize 2 Timothy 2:25–26 so that you can use it often in prayer, as demonstrated on page 16.

"God is in CONTROL" Thats when I prayed stormy

The Lord Who Is Worthy
to Be Called On

From the Fall to the Flood

By God's grace, it has been my practice throughout my Christian life to maintain a consistent prayer life. I didn't begin with a method, but over the years I have developed one. I have a stack of index cards categorized by subjects that I pray through every morning while I exercise. Recognizing that Scripture must inform our prayers, some cards contain a prayer from Scripture or an answer to a catechism question that can be used as a prayer. One card lists persecuted countries, political leaders, and a child our family sponsors through Compassion International. Others contain names of missionaries and church plants. Various others bear the names of pastors, elders, deacons, and a number of people and organizations engaged in biblical education. I also include friends, acquaintances, and neighbors, along with their special needs. One has the names of my extended family. And then I have a separate card for my husband and for each of my children.

At night I use a prayer journal containing lists of people who have either asked me to pray for them or whose prayer needs I have learned of through our encounters. It has the prayer requests of the women in my Bible study group. I also use it to write out longer prayers concerning matters on my heart.

Why do I take prayer seriously? I make time for prayer because I firmly believe, by God's grace, that I am speaking to the Lord whose name is worthy to be called on. For believers, one of the greatest privileges is to be able to talk with God. I'm deeply aware that I wouldn't be able to pray except for my beloved Lord and Savior opening the way to the throne of my Father through His death on the cross.

What we say to God should be in response to what He has said to us through the Scriptures. The story of the Bible must inform our prayers. It guides us into truth so that we can pray in a way that honors the Lord. As the story of Scripture unfolds, we come to learn different aspects of prayer. In the last chapter, we looked at the story of creation and the fall and learned that the Lord calls to His people. He takes the initiative to talk to us. In this chapter we will learn about the Lord whose name is worthy to be called on through the story of Noah and the flood.

To Whom Will We Turn?

Eve had experienced the consequences of her sin when she endured pain in bearing Cain and then later Abel, but the pain of childbirth didn't compare with that of losing a child, especially when it was at the hand of her other son. Sin was crouching at the door of Cain's heart, as it did for his mother and father, and instead of listening to God, Cain listened to the father of lies. In his anger and envy, he killed his brother, Abel. God questioned Cain, just as he had questioned Adam and Eve. This was Cain's opportunity to repent and confess. The Lord asked, "Where is Abel your brother?" (Gen. 4:9). But instead of repenting, he refused to take responsibility for his sin, answering, "I do not know. Am I my brother's keeper?" (v. 9). Because Cain refused to cry out to the Lord in repentance, his brother's blood cried out for the Lord's judgment (vv. 10–11).

The storyline of Cain and Abel is referenced in the book of Hebrews. Because of the atoning work of Jesus Christ, believers "have come to Mount Zion and to the city of the living God…to God the Judge of all…to Jesus the Mediator of the new covenant, *and to the blood of sprinkling that speaks better things than that of Abel*" (Heb. 12:22–24). Abel's blood cried out for justice; Jesus's blood cried out for grace and mercy. God set His Son "forth as a propitiation by

His blood, through faith, to demonstrate His righteousness, because in His forbearance God had passed over the sins that were previously committed, to demonstrate at the present time His righteousness, that He might be just and the justifier of the one who has faith in Jesus" (Rom. 3:25–26). Don't be like Cain and refuse to repent of your sin and take responsibility for it. Call on the name of the Lord. His ears are open wide to those who call to Him in faith. He stands ready to hear and forgive.

The cure for sin would not come through Cain. He was cast away from the presence of the Lord. And Abel, the one who had pleased the Lord with his offering, was now dead. What of the promised Seed who would come through the woman to crush the head of the serpent? In time, God gave Eve another son, Seth, and Seth also had a son, Enosh. At that time "men began to call on the name of the LORD" (Gen. 4:26). God's promise would not be thwarted. He would indeed raise up a Seed of the woman to crush the head of the serpent.

His Name Is Worthy

It is a wonder that the Lord revealed Himself to His people so that they could call on Him by name. Adam was not able to keep the covenant of works. He had failed miserably. The stipulations of the covenant of works—perfect obedience—would have to be fulfilled by the second Adam through the covenant of grace. This covenant of grace rested on the more foundational covenant of redemption. The covenant of redemption was made before the creation of the world between the three persons of the Godhead. The Father appointed the plan of redemption, the Son accomplished it, and the Holy Spirit applies the benefits of redemption to every one of God's children.

This triune God wants to be known by name. That is why He condescended to His people by way of covenant. The covenant-keeping God revealed Himself to His people. Seth would have heard from his parents that God is the Creator of all things. He would have been told about their conversations in Eden. How much Adam and Eve had learned about God! They had been perfect in knowledge, righteousness, and holiness. When they sinned, they didn't forget God's name. They passed along to the next generation that the Creator God is also the covenant God.

Adam and Eve had also learned that God is the Judge. They had heard the Judge's voice pronounce the curse on the serpent and the consequences for their sin. And they knew that He was holy. He could not dwell with sinners, so He had sent them out of the garden. They also knew that He was a God of grace. He had not killed Adam and Eve on the spot. He had promised to raise up a Seed of seeds to crush Satan's head.

By God's grace, God's people had learned that His name was worthy to be called on. Have you called on Him? As you have listened to God's word preached on Sundays, as you have witnessed His work in your life as well as in the lives of those around you, as you have studied the Scriptures, have you learned that God's name is worthy for you to call on in prayer? When anger and envy fill your heart and you're tempted to murder your friend, spouse, or sister in Christ with your words (Matt. 5:21–22), have you learned to call on the Lord? Sometimes it might be a quick, quiet plea: *Help! I'm about to say something I know I shouldn't say or do something I know I shouldn't do. I need your strength to stop!* But I hope that more often than not, you set aside some time to pray to the Lord, who has allowed us to call Him by name. His name is worthy to be called on. It should be on our lips often as we call to Him in prayer, standing in awe of His attributes, humbling ourselves before Him, thanking Him for His gifts, and pleading with Him for growth in godliness, both for ourselves and for others.

A Man Who Found Grace

Another important event in redemptive history that informs our life of prayer is God's covenant with Noah. God's covenant with Noah does not stand apart from the one overarching covenant of grace established in Genesis 3:15, but instead is a further unfolding of what the covenant of grace entails. Noah was a descendant of Adam and Seth, and his story is told in Genesis 6–9. The name Noah sounds like the Hebrew word for "rest," and Noah's father gave him that name because he believed his son would bring humankind relief from the difficult work and painful toil resulting from God's curse (Gen. 5:29). It's likely that whenever Noah's father heard or spoke his son's name, he would long for the rest that he believed would come through his child.

It was during Noah's lifetime that the Lord decided He wanted rest from humankind. He was grieved over how evil His creatures' hearts had become, so He decided to destroy all people, animals, creeping things, and birds by a flood: "And the LORD was sorry that He had made man on the earth, and He was grieved in His heart. So the LORD said, 'I will destroy man whom I have created from the face of the earth'" (Gen. 6:6–7). This is what was expected when Adam and Eve sinned. Now it had finally come. The punishment of death because of sin would fall on humankind.

But amazingly, the Lord preserved a remnant. He wasn't going to destroy Noah. "But Noah found grace in the eyes of the LORD" (Gen. 6:8). It wasn't because Noah was sinless that God saved him, as becomes clear later in the narrative when his fall into drunkenness leads to serious consequences (9:20–25). God saved him because He is gracious. He would use Noah to point people to the sinless One. God also spared Noah's wife, his sons and his daughters-in-law, as well as pairs of clean and unclean animals and birds. Although the Lord would bring judgment on the earth by a flood, He would save this remnant by way of an ark. The Lord told Noah exactly how to build the ark that would preserve him and his family, and Noah obeyed. "Thus Noah did; according to all that God commanded him, so he did" (Gen. 6:22).

During the long dark days and nights of the flood, the Lord preserved Noah and his family, along with the animals, on the ark. As soon as the Lord told Noah to exit the ark, Noah worshiped the One who had preserved his life. He built an altar, took some of the animals that had been with him on the ark, and offered burnt offerings to the Lord. At that time God made a covenant with Noah and his future offspring. The Lord promised that as long as the earth remains, seedtime and harvest, cold and heat, summer and winter, and day and night will continue (Gen. 8:22). God's covenant with Noah also promised that though the righteous will be saved, the wicked will be judged (9:1–27). Through this covenant we learn several important things about the God to whom we pray.

He Is the Creator

When we pray, we are speaking to the Creator of the heavens and the earth. God made the ground and has the authority to promise never to curse it again or to strike down every living creature (Gen. 8:21). When you're fighting to understand your identity; believing lies about your appearance; or tempted to think the storm, hurricane, or tornado is greater than the Creator, remember Noah's God is our God, the Creator of the heavens and the earth.

In telling the Colossians about the kingdom of God's beloved Son, in whom we have redemption and the forgiveness of sins, Paul teaches that God created all things through Christ and for Christ. He is before all things. And in Christ all things hold together: "For it pleased the Father that in Him all the fullness should dwell, and by Him to reconcile all things to Himself, by Him, whether things on earth or things in heaven, having made peace through the blood of His cross" (Col. 1:19–20). When we pray to the Creator God, we speak to the triune God. We have the privilege to pray to God the Father through Christ the Son by the power of the Holy Spirit.

He Is the Sustainer

God's covenant with Noah also teaches us that we pray to the Sustainer who upholds seedtime and harvest, cold and heat, summer and winter, and day and night (Gen. 8:22). We pray in the context of an ordained rhythm, talking to God throughout different seasons and years. This is true both literally and figuratively. We pray from spring, to summer, to fall, to winter. We pray from morning to evening. We also pray through different seasons of life, such as when we are students, single, and married and during motherhood and widowhood.

When the apostle Paul addressed the men of Athens, he said, "God, who made the world and everything in it, since He is Lord of heaven and earth, does not dwell in temples made with hands. Nor is He worshiped with men's hands, as though He needed anything, since He gives to all life, breath, and all things. And He has made from one blood every nation of men to dwell on all the face of the earth, and has determined their preappointed times and the boundaries of their dwellings" (Acts 17:24–26). This passage combines the truths that God is both Creator and Sustainer. We don't come before God in prayer because He needs us to sustain Him. We don't enter His presence because He needs us to give Him anything. We don't bow before Him to tell Him what we have decided is best for our life. No, the Creator God is self-sustaining. He doesn't need us. But we desperately need Him. We come to Him in prayer because we need His sustaining power, His presence, and His gifts of breath and life. We need His divine orchestration of our preappointed times and the boundaries of our dwellings. And amazingly, He gives these things to us out of His free grace and love.

He Is the Provider

Another aspect of prayer that we learn through God's covenant with Noah is that we pray to the Provider who gives food to His people (Gen. 9:3). Noah and his family had been eating green plants, but now they could eat meat from animals. The Lord delights to take care of His children by giving them the good gift of food.

When Jesus was preaching His Sermon on the Mount, He told His disciples not to be anxious about food and clothing. Instead, they were to observe how their heavenly Father fed the birds and clothed the flowers of the field and seek after the kingdom of God (Matt. 6:25–33). Jesus taught His disciples to pray for food (v. 11), so it is good and right for us to ask God to provide for our daily needs. As we do so, we can be certain that the Lord who gave food to Noah and his family gives food to His people today. Are you concerned about where next week's groceries are going to come from? Is the clothing budget running tight? Does it seem like you're always

pinching pennies at the store and cabinets are growing bare? Stop
and pray right now to the Lord who provides, asking Him to supply
your needs.

He Is Our Rest

God's covenant with Noah also highlights that we pray to the God
who has provided rest for us (Gen. 9:11–17). The sign of the covenant, the rainbow, shines brightly against the dark storm clouds in
the sky. Each time Noah and his offspring saw the rainbow, they
would recall the covenant God had spoken and remember that they
have a relationship with the One who gives rest to His people. And
each time the Lord saw the rainbow, He would remember to make
good on His word.

The Creator "God who commanded light to shine out of darkness, who has shone in our hearts to give the light of the knowledge
of the glory of God in the face of Jesus Christ" (2 Cor. 4:6) knows that
we are jars of clay. He knows that we need rest and relief as we live in
this fallen world. And He has given it to us in Christ. Whatever our
weakness, it is to show "that the excellence of the power may be of
God and not of us" (v. 7).

There is a rest for the people of God through faith in Jesus Christ.
Noah could not give God's people the rest his father longed for, but
the greater and final Noah has. When Noah's father named him,
he never could have imagined that a descendant of his son would
provide eternal rest. Christ alone can fulfill Lamech's words: "This
one will comfort us concerning our work and the toil of our hands,
because of the ground which the LORD has cursed" (Gen. 5:29).

Paul says,

> The creation eagerly waits for the revealing of the sons of God.
> For the creation was subjected to futility, not willingly, but
> because of Him who subjected it in hope; because the creation
> itself also will be delivered from the bondage of corruption
> into the glorious liberty of the children of God. For we know
> that the whole creation groans and labors with birth pangs
> together until now. Not only that, but we also who have the

firstfruits of the Spirit, even we ourselves groan within ourselves, eagerly waiting for the adoption, the redemption of our body. (Rom. 8:19–23)

The author of Hebrews says, "For he who has entered His rest [through Christ] has himself also ceased from his works as God did from His" (4:10).

This rest will be consummated at Christ's return when we will stand around the throne of God and of the Lamb, which in John's vision is surrounded by a rainbow, to worship Him (Rev. 4:3; 22:3). We will see the face of our beloved Lord and Savior, and night will be no more, nor will we need the sun because the Lord God will be our light (22:4–5).

If we're going to spend an eternity talking to God, don't you want to start now? Since He is our Creator, Sustainer, Provider, and rest, don't you want to run to Him first thing in the morning, last thing at night, and many times in between to tell Him how great He is, to ask Him to sustain you and provide for you, and to thank Him that you have rest in Him?

* * * * *

By God's grace, I love to call on His name because He first called me by name. He made me His child and gave me the privilege of praying. We can call on the name of the Lord anytime and anywhere. We can have our eyes open or closed. We can be on our knees or exercising. We can be driving or doing dishes. We can be lying down or standing up. What matters is that we pray. For the believer, prayer isn't a suggestion, but a command. "Rejoice always, pray without ceasing, in everything give thanks; for this is the will of God in Christ Jesus for you" (1 Thess. 5:16–18).

Time to Ponder and Pray

1. Describe your prayer life. What are some ways you could add structure to it? What might that look like for your day? If you like the idea of index cards, try making a stack this week with labels at the top like the ones mentioned at the beginning of this chapter.

2. Cain's envy and anger got him in trouble. Instead of calling on the name of the Lord, he remained unrepentant of his sin. In what way(s) is sin crouching at the door of your heart? Take time now to repent of your sin and run to Christ, asking Him to help you hate it and forsake it.

3. In the midst of your present circumstances, how does it comfort you that God's promises cannot be thwarted?

4. How are you teaching those under your influence that the Lord's name is worthy to be called on? Give an example of a time this week when you cried out to the Lord. How does your prayer life reflect that you stand in awe of God's attributes, humble yourself before Him, thank Him for His gifts, and plead with Him for growth in godliness for yourself and others?

5. Why is it helpful to think about the importance of the redemptive-historical markers in Scripture? Why does it help to think about prayer in the context of these markers?

6. The first thing Noah did when he got off the ark was build an altar to the Lord to offer burnt offerings. Although we don't build altars anymore and offer burnt offerings, the author of Hebrews

exhorts us to "continually offer the sacrifice of praise to God, that is, the fruit of our lips, giving thanks to His name" (13:15). How are you doing this, and how are you leading those under your care to do this on a continual basis? Take a moment now to acknowledge God's name in prayer.

7. How does the truth that God is the Creator of all things impact how you pray? How does the truth that God is the Sustainer inform your prayers? How does the truth that the Lord provides for His people inform your prayers? How have these truths impacted your prayers recently?

8. How could you use the things you've learned about God in His covenant with Noah as an outline for prayer in your life, as well as in the lives of those you teach?

9. In light of what you've learned in this chapter, write out a prayer to God.

10. Seek to memorize 1 Thessalonians 5:16–18.

3

The God Who Is Faithful

From the Flood to the Patriarchs

In your most trying moments, to whom do you turn? During the stressful nights as a student, the loneliness of singleness, the dark days of marriage, the heartache of motherhood, the chaos of your career, the stress of aging parents, or the pain that takes your breath away, to whom do you go for help? If you're like me, you want to go to someone who has proven to be faithful as a friend, neighbor, pastor, or family member. But as faithful as these people might be, their faithfulness pales in comparison to God's faithfulness. And in our most trying moments we need the One who is most faithful. He is the one we must go to first to help us in our time of need.

One of the most difficult days in my life was in January 2009 when I was seized with severe abdominal pain. Within a matter of hours I went from standing to crouching over to writhing on the floor in pain. The ambulance ride was horrific. The person attending me heard me send up a lot of repeated cries: "Oh God, help me!" In the blinding pain, distress, and fear of death, that is all I could scream. But I didn't need more eloquence or lengthier prayers. The faithful God heard me.

Do you, dear reader, know that the God who invites you to talk to Him in prayer is faithful to keep His promises? Do you know that He is faithful to be present with you, protect you, provide for you, and give you His peace? When the opposition is too oppressive, the distress too disillusioning, the pain too pulverizing, fix your eyes on the faithful One and cry out to Him.

In the last two chapters we have traced the theme of prayer from creation to the fall, examining Adam and Eve's relationship with the Lord in Eden; and then from the fall to the flood, looking at when people in Seth's line began calling on the name of the Lord. We took a long look at how God's covenant with Noah reveals certain aspects of prayer. Now we come to the patriarchal period, which spans the time from Abraham to Moses. In the patriarchal narratives we will learn that the God who calls to His people and is worthy to be called on is faithful.

God's Covenant with Abraham

Although we won't be examining God's covenant with Abraham as fully as we would if this book was a biblical theology of covenants, it's important that we acknowledge God's covenant with Abraham is an important redemptive-historical marker in Scripture and note a few important things about it. The crux of the covenant of grace can be summed up in one phrase: "I will walk among you and be your God, and you shall be My people" (Lev. 26:12). So first, God promised Abraham His presence, "to be God to you and your descendants after you.... And I will be their God" (Gen. 17:7–8). Second, God promised Abraham a people; God would make him a great nation (12:2; 17:4–6). Third, God promised Abraham a possession; He would give His people the land of Canaan (12:7; 13:14–17; 15:18–21; 17:8). Fourth, God promised Abraham that He had a bigger purpose than he could ever imagine. The nation that came through his seed was to point others to the Lord so that all the families of the earth would be blessed (12:3). We cannot understand the prayers of the patriarchs without recalling God's covenant with Abraham, which was later renewed with Isaac and Jacob, because it serves as the foundation for their prayers.[1]

---

1. E. P. Clowney, "Prayer," *New Dictionary of Biblical Theology*, ed. T. Desmond

The Lord Has Made Me Rich

An interesting story occurs in Genesis 14 between God making several promises to Abraham in Genesis 12 but before formalizing them in a covenant in chapter 15. Abraham had just returned victorious from a battle, and the king of Sodom and Melchizedek, king of Salem and priest of God Most High, went out to meet him at the King's Valley (Gen. 14:17–24). The king of Sodom told Abraham to give him the people captured in battle but to keep the goods for himself. Abraham told the king of Sodom no because he had vowed to the Lord that he wouldn't take anything from the king, lest he claim that he had made Abraham rich (v. 23). Abraham trusted in God's faithfulness to His promises. He wanted others who saw his wealth to say that the Lord had made him rich.

The king-priest of Salem, Melchizedek, blessed Abraham in the name of God Most High, possessor of heaven and earth, and attributed Abraham's victory to Him (Gen. 14:19–20). This pleased Abraham, which is why he gave Melchizedek a tenth of everything. In his conversation with these two kings, Abraham used God's personal name Yahweh alongside God Most High, possessor of heaven and earth. He had lifted his hand to the Lord and made a promise to Him. There is no other name in heaven or on earth that is greater than Yahweh, the covenant God. The God to whom we pray is most high. He is possessor of heaven and earth.

The author of Hebrews refers to this king-priest of Salem when he writes about Jesus:

> In the days of His flesh, when He had offered up prayers and supplications, with vehement cries and tears to Him who was able to save Him from death, and was heard because of His godly fear, though He was a Son, yet He learned obedience by the things which He suffered. And having been perfected, He became the author of eternal salvation to all who obey Him, called by God as High Priest "according to the order of Melchizedek." (Heb. 5:7–10)

Alexander, Brian S. Rosner, D. A. Carson, and Graeme Goldsworthy (Downers Grove, Ill.: IVP Academic, 2000), 692.

Because Jesus, the greater priest than Melchizedek, became the author of salvation to all who obey Him, you and I are incredibly rich. Believers have been blessed with "every spiritual blessing" (Eph. 1:3). In Christ "we have redemption through His blood, the forgiveness of sins" and "have obtained an inheritance" that is guaranteed by the Holy Spirit (1:7, 11, 13–14). Such riches remind us that when the bank account is nearly empty, friendships seem to be lacking, and resources seem far away, we can (and should!) rejoice before our heavenly Father in prayer, thanking Him for the riches that are already ours in Christ Jesus.

How Do I Know He Will Be Faithful?

Immediately before the account of God's covenant with Abraham, we read a beautiful interpersonal exchange between the Lord and Abraham. The Lord initiated and Abraham responded. The Lord told Abraham not to fear because He was his shield, and his reward would be great. Abraham responded by asking, "Lord GOD, what will You give me, seeing I go childless, and the heir of my house is Eliezer of Damascus?… Look, You have given me no offspring; indeed one born in my house is my heir.… Lord GOD, how shall I know that I will inherit it?" (Gen. 15:2–3, 8).

You have been in Abraham's shoes, haven't you? You have read all the promises of Scripture. You have heard sermon after sermon. You have read every book and resource there is on the topic. But you still cry out, *O Lord, You have not given me what I need for You to accomplish Your purposes in my life. How will I know You will do it?* You wonder if God will pull you through that difficult class in graduate school. You question what He is doing by keeping you single. You think that somewhere along the line you messed up and can't fix things. You wonder if your job is going to provide. You fear your marriage won't make it. You cry out, *O Lord, how do I know You're going to come through for me?*

In between Abraham's heartfelt cries to the Lord, the Lord spoke. His presence was known and His promises declared. Abraham's prayer didn't go unanswered. The Lord God heard. He knew

Abraham by name, and Abraham knew Him by name. The Lord speaks to you too. He has spoken to you in the Scriptures. He has spoken to you by His Son. He is with you right now. His promises are for you. Your cries for help won't go unanswered.

When God told Abraham that he and Sarah would have a son, Abraham laughed to himself. After all, he was one hundred years old, and Sarah was ninety! Abraham suggested that his son Ishmael, whom he had with Sarah's servant Hagar, could be the heir (Gen. 17:17–18). Again, Scripture gives a personal exchange between Abraham and God. God told Abraham no. Abraham's idea wasn't in accord with God's plan, which was to bring Isaac (meaning "laughter") into the world through this barren couple. The narrative says, "Then He finished talking with him, and God went up from Abraham" (v. 22). Amazing! God had come down to talk with Abraham. This personal relationship that God had with the patriarchs reveals once again that God wants to have a warm, intimate relationship with His people without ever minimizing that He is God Most High, bringing His plans and purposes to pass.

A Bold Request

Not only could Abraham ask the Lord questions, but he could also intercede for others. News of Sodom's sin had reached heaven. The Lord was going to investigate. And the life of every person in Sodom was at risk of being destroyed if He found it to be true. Abraham stood before the Lord and questioned His justice: "Shall not the Judge of all the earth do right?" (Gen. 18:25). Abraham couldn't believe God was going to sweep away the righteous with the wicked. Even though he knew he was "but dust and ashes" (v. 27), Abraham continued to boldly ask the Lord to spare the city on account of the righteous in it. He started by proposing that the Lord spare the city if fifty righteous people were found in it and worked all the way down to ten. Each time the Lord agreed to Abraham's proposal. Then "the LORD went His way as soon as He had finished speaking with Abraham; and Abraham returned to his place" (Gen. 18:33). You may recall that the

Lord did destroy Sodom, but He remembered Abraham's intercessory prayer and saved Lot (Gen. 19:29).

Such intercessory prayer anticipates a greater intercessor. Except for Jesus Christ interceding on our behalf, we would be destroyed like the inhabitants of Sodom. There is no one righteous. "All have sinned and fall short of the glory of God" (Rom. 3:23). The Judge of all the earth would be just in destroying all humankind because of our sin. But Jesus Christ took the judgment of God's people on Himself. Now He intercedes for us as our Great High Priest. He is the one who will judge the living and the dead at His return. There is no other name by which to be saved. Now is the time to pray, *O Lord God, I know that I am a sinner in need of grace. I repent of my sins. I need You as my Savior. And I want to follow You as Lord. In Jesus's name I pray, amen.* If you are already a believer, for whom do you need to intercede, asking the Lord to save them from destruction?

The story of Abraham's intercession for the righteous in Sodom reveals another important redemptive-historical point. As wonderful as it is to read the interchanges between the Lord and Abraham, the Lord was not always with Abraham. The Lord went His way, and Abraham went his way (Gen. 18:33). The patriarchal narratives leave us longing for more permanent fellowship with the Lord—uninterrupted fellowship. These sporadic conversations point down the corridor of Scripture, begging for a solution. What if Abraham could talk to God anytime, anywhere? Would that ever be possible? This tension, though lessened when the tabernacle and later the temple were erected, would not be resolved until the true temple came who is not made with human hands.

Jesus inaugurated a time in redemptive history when we don't have to go to a certain place to speak with God or wait for a certain time; we can worship God in spirit and truth anytime and anywhere (John 4:23–24). Since the Spirit of God indwells believers, we are temples of the Holy Spirit. Whereas the Jews had to travel to the temple in Jerusalem to worship, the true temple, Jesus Christ, traveled from heaven to earth so that God's people would not have to travel to worship Him. We take the temple with us everywhere we go. This doesn't negate the importance of gathering for corporate worship on the Lord's Day, of course (Heb. 10:25), but it helps us understand the privilege we have as believers under the new covenant. Abraham spoke sporadically with the Lord; we can converse continually.

Where He Leads Me, I Will Follow

It wasn't just Abraham who talked with God. In Genesis 24 we learn that Abraham's servant also had a relationship with the Lord. Abraham gave him the task of finding a wife for Isaac. He did not want Isaac to marry a Canaanite, so he sent his servant to his country and family with the promise that the Lord would send His angel before him to help him. When the servant reached the city of Nahor in Mesopotamia, he prayed to the Lord, asking Him to grant him success and to show steadfast love to Abraham by leading him to the woman for Isaac to marry (Gen. 24:12–14). When the Lord answered his prayer by sending Rebekah, the servant bowed his head in worship and prayed again, acknowledging the steadfast love and faithfulness of the Lord, who had led him to Isaac's wife (vv. 26–27). Here again the aspect of prayer that is highlighted is that God is a personal God who wants to be involved in His people's lives. He is faithful and steadfast in love. He leads and guides His people. When His people call on Him, He hears and answers.

If you're like me, you still want the Lord to answer your prayers in the way He responded to the servant's prayer. How I longed for a postcard in the mail telling me which seminary the Lord wanted me to attend, or the man He wanted me to marry, or the ministry position He wanted me to fill. How I agonized over big decisions like these! As the story of Scripture unfolds, we learn that God does delight in leading His children, but He doesn't do so in the same way that He led Abraham's servant to Isaac's wife. We pray and ask God for wisdom. We ask others to pray for us. We consult Scripture. Then we step out in faith, trusting in God's sovereignty and providence. Prayer is the solution to paralysis in decision-making. We don't have to fear we'll mess up something, such as God's plan for our lives!

Martin Luther Reformation

Don't worry. We can't mess up God's plan for our lives. Pray for wisdom. Pray with others. Pursue godly counsel. Plan wisely. Practice biblical principles. Put your trust in God. He is faithful to keep you within His plans and purposes for your life.

God's Covenant Grounds Our Prayers

The covenant that God made with Abraham was reaffirmed with his son Isaac. The Lord appeared to Isaac in Beersheba, revealing Himself as "the God of your father Abraham" and telling him, "Do not fear, for I am with you. I will bless you and multiply your descendants for My servant Abraham's sake" (Gen. 26:24). In response, Isaac built an altar and called on the name of the Lord. Here again God's covenant is the foundation of prayer. God initiated a relationship with Isaac. He is a personal God who wants to know His people and invites them to know Him and call on His name. His faithfulness to the covenant He made with Abraham is displayed through His relationship with Isaac, and Isaac responded in faith.

God's covenant with Abraham was also reaffirmed with his grandson Jacob through a dream: "A ladder was set up on the earth, and its top reached to heaven; and there the angels of God were ascending and descending on it" (Gen. 28:12). The Lord stood beside Jacob in the dream and promised him what He had promised Abraham and had then reaffirmed with Isaac. Jacob recognized after he awoke that the presence of God had been with him (vv. 10–17). He made a vow, saying that if God's presence, protection, provision, and peace would be with him, then "the LORD shall be my God" (v. 21). Jacob's dream reveals an important characteristic of prayer. God is present with His people. We don't pray to a God who is far away or even in another room, but to One who is beside us. The Lord God comes down to His people.

Jesus alluded to Jacob's dream in his conversation with Nathanael in John 1:51. Jesus's disciple Philip encouraged his friend Nathanael to come see Jesus. Nathanael was amazed when Jesus revealed that He knew him and had seen him under a fig tree (vv. 45–49). Nathanael believed in Jesus as the Son of God, the King of Israel.

Jesus told Nathanael that he would see even greater things: "Most assuredly, I say to you, hereafter you shall see heaven open, and the angels of God ascending and descending upon the Son of Man" (John 1:51). In other words, Jesus says that He is the ladder Jacob once saw that bridges the gap between heaven and earth. No one can pray to the Father except through the Son. Jacob knew God's presence beside him, but we know God's presence within us. Jacob knew His presence when God appeared to him, but we know His presence always.

God Listens to Us When We Pray

Another important aspect of prayer we learn from the life of Jacob comes in the narrative concerning his children. Jacob had two wives, Leah and Rachel. Rachel experienced infertility. Although Scripture doesn't record her prayers for a son, we know she prayed: "Then God remembered Rachel, *and God listened to her* and opened her womb" (Gen. 30:22). What a precious phrase! Perhaps you, dear reader, know the pain of infertility. Or maybe you know the heartache of longing for a husband but not having that desire fulfilled. There are many people, places, and things for which we long and pray, but we wonder deep down if God hears us, especially if our prayer seems to go unanswered. Take heart! While God's answer to Rachel's prayer isn't a promise for everyone that the Lord will deliver what we ask for, it is a promise that God listens to us. He hears our longings that we lay before Him in prayer, and He answers. We can be certain that whether He says no, wait, or yes, He is good and faithful in bringing His purposes to pass in our lives.

The Lord Hears Our Fear and Distress

One of the most significant events in Jacob's life is recorded in Genesis 27, when Isaac, close to death, prepared to bless Esau, the firstborn of the twin brothers. But Rebekah had devised a crafty plan to trick her husband into blessing Jacob instead of Esau, and sadly, Jacob went along with the plan. Esau then hated Jacob because he had stolen the blessing and threatened to kill him after Isaac died. Rebekah told Jacob to flee to her brother Laban's home in Haran until Esau's anger subsided, and Jacob did. In Haran he worked for Laban and married Laban's daughters, Leah and Rachel. After many years of shepherding Laban's flocks, Jacob acquired great wealth for himself. Laban's sons were jealous of him, and Laban no longer showed him the same favor. So the Lord instructed Jacob to return home and promised His presence would accompany him (Gen. 31:1–3).

It had been many years since Jacob had seen Esau. He remembered well how angry Esau had been when he had fled from home. So he sent messengers ahead to find favor in Esau's eyes. The messengers returned to tell Jacob that Esau was coming to meet him with four hundred men, which made Jacob very afraid. He assumed Esau's rage was as hot as it was on the day he had left. He quickly divided the people who were with him so that if Esau attacked one group, the other group would have time to escape.

In his distress he cried out to the Lord:

> O God of my father Abraham and God of my father Isaac, the LORD who said to me, "Return to your country and to your family, and I will deal well with you": I am not worthy of the least of all the mercies and of all the truth which You have shown Your servant; for I crossed over this Jordan with my staff, and now I have become two companies. Deliver me, I pray, from the hand of my brother, from the hand of Esau; for I fear him, lest he come and attack me and the mother with the children. For You said, "I will surely treat you well, and make your descendants as the sand of the sea, which cannot be numbered for multitude." (Gen. 32:9–12)

You can almost hear Jacob's heartfelt cry, can't you? This is a man who was anxious and afraid, but instead of turning to his own resources or to those of others, he turned to God and cried out to Him for help in time of need.

From this longest prayer that has been recorded from the patriarchal period, we are reminded that we pray to a personal God, as Jacob did. This is the same God who had revealed Himself to Jacob's father and grandfather as well as to Jacob. This is the covenant Lord who initiated a relationship with His people. This is the God who had stood beside Jacob in his dream. In his prayer, Jacob reminded the Lord of His instructions to him. He was obeying God in returning home, but now it didn't seem like a good idea. Scripture invites us to remind the Lord in our prayers, of the promises and precepts He has given to us. Jacob also teaches us that we must approach the Lord with humility. Here, Jacob humbly approached the Lord and acknowledged that he wasn't worthy of the Lord's steadfast love and faithfulness. When we are anxious and afraid, we too can turn to the personal God in a posture of humility, asking for deliverance and reminding God of His promises to us in His word. When Jacob asked God for deliverance from harm while acknowledging his fear of Esau, he modeled boldness and authenticity in prayer. And when Jacob reminded the Lord of His covenant promises, recognizing that if the Lord didn't save his family from Esau, then his offspring certainly wouldn't be numerous, he gave us an example of using God's promises as the foundation of our prayers.

The Lord Forgives

During this time of distress, when Jacob knew that Esau was coming toward him with four hundred men, he feared for his life and the lives of his loved ones. He sent his two wives, two female servants, eleven children, and everything else he had ahead of him so that he was left alone. During the night, a man wrestled with him until dawn. Jacob did not let the man prevail against him, but he was injured in the wrestling match. The man touched Jacob's hip socket and put it out of joint. The man told Jacob to let him go, but Jacob refused, insisting that the man bless him. This "man" was God Himself! He changed Jacob's name to Israel because he had striven with God and men and prevailed. When Jacob asked the man His name, He questioned why Jacob asked and then blessed him. Jacob knew that he had seen God face-to-face, yet his life was spared (Gen. 32:22–30).

Jacob's restless night wrestling with the Lord and insisting on a blessing anticipates the Canaanite woman who prevailed with

Jesus, asking for His mercy on her daughter, who was oppressed by a demon (Matt. 15:22–28). Jesus's answer that He was sent only to the lost sheep of Israel didn't stop her. She pleaded for His help. Again, He refused. But she prevailed in faith. Then Jesus answered, "O woman, great is your faith! Let it be to you as you desire" (v. 28).

But there's more! Hosea 12:2–4 comments on this event in Jacob's life:

> The LORD also brings a charge against Judah,
> And will punish Jacob according to his ways;
> According to his deeds He will recompense him.
> He took his brother by the heel in the womb,
> And in his strength he struggled with God.
> Yes, he struggled with the Angel and prevailed;
> He wept, and sought favor from Him.

In the context of Hosea, God reminded the people of Israel of Jacob's story as an example of their history of rebellion and their need of repentance. Jacob's night of wrestling was both physical and spiritual. He was hardly the poster child of godliness. Of the three patriarchs, he is portrayed as the least godly. But during his wrestling match, he had come to recognize his sin and sought God's favor.[2]

Prayer isn't magic. We can't depend on our tactics or use our best wrestling moves to get what we want from the Lord. Neither Jacob's story nor the story of the Canaanite woman's faith teaches that. In both cases the person called on the name of the Lord. The Lord's name is not like yours and mine. It stands for His character. He is faithful to accomplish His good purposes in our lives, and because of His faithfulness we have every reason to persevere in prayer.

There is probably someone who needs you to struggle for them in prayer. Perhaps it's so that her heart may be encouraged, or that her unity with others would be strengthened, or that her understanding and knowledge of Christ would grow (Col. 2:1–2). Maybe it's so that she may stand mature and fully assured in all the will of God (Col. 4:12). Perhaps this person needs to be delivered from an

---

2. Vos, *Biblical Theology*, 97–99.

addiction or anger, depression or disillusionment, poverty or pain, unbelief or unruliness. Prevail in prayer on her behalf. Don't give up. Cry out to the Lord for her deliverance. And then rest in His sovereignty and goodness.

It may also be that you should prevail in prayer because you need the Lord's forgiveness and favor. Perhaps you, like Jacob, have been deceitful and rebellious. Maybe you are in desperate need of God's forgiveness for a specific sin. Perhaps your communion with Him in prayer has been broken because you refuse to repent of your anger, envy, greed, or sexual immorality. We don't have to wrestle with God in prayer the same way Jacob did. But his story encourages us to seek God's grace in the wake of our sin.

> So you, by the help of your God, return;
> Observe mercy and justice,
> And wait on your God continually. (Hos. 12:6)

Affirm His Faithfulness

As the narrative of Jacob's life draws to a close in Genesis 35, the Lord instructed him to return to Bethel, the place where he had dreamed about the ladder, and make an altar to the Lord. Remember that Jacob's faith in God was conditional at that point. He bargained with God, saying, "If You'll be present with me, protect me, provide for me, and grant me peace, then You will be my God." Jacob's vow implied that if God failed at any one of these points, he wouldn't follow Him. Now God gave him another opportunity to affirm His faithfulness. The Lord had shown Himself faithful in Jacob's life. He had been present with him and protected him. He provided for him and granted him peace with Esau.

When Jacob arrived at Bethel for the second time, God once again appeared to him and blessed him. He called his name Israel and reaffirmed the covenant promises He had given to Abraham and Isaac. "Then God went up from him in the place where He talked with him" (Gen. 35:13). Jacob made an altar and poured out a drink offering on it. He affirmed God's faithfulness.

It would take a greater Israel than this one to secure a prayer life for a people God would never leave. In the fullness of time, the true Israel would come. In His distress and with an enemy far greater than Esau threatening Him, Jesus prevailed in prayer in Gethsemane and over the powers of darkness on the cross so that God's presence might take up residence in our hearts. When He ascended into heaven, He sent His Spirit, who helps us prevail in prayer (Rom. 8:26–27). Without His help, we would be like the disciples in Gethsemane, falling asleep when we should be praying. But the Spirit helps us in our weakness. Is your prayer life weak? Do you lack faith in God's faithfulness? He is near to you and ready to listen now. Go ahead and speak. He delights to hear His people pray.

* * * * *

I hope that in your most trying moments you turn to the Lord. When you're tempted during depressing days and dark nights or in loneliness, heartache, chaos, stress, or physical pain to turn to someone other than the Lord, don't. It's good and right to have faithful Christian friends to encourage us and uphold us in prayer. But turn to Christ first. No one can compare to Him in faithfulness.

Time to Ponder and Pray

1. Describe a recent situation in which you needed help. Did you turn to the Lord first, or did you turn to a friend? After reading this chapter, what do you think is the better approach? Explain why it would be a good idea for you to invite your sisters in Christ to help you, beginning with prayer.

2. In what situation are you crying out, *O Lord, You have not given me what I need for You to accomplish Your purposes in my life?*

How will I know You will do it? How does God's word to Abraham strengthen your faith?

3. Describe a time when you have acknowledged yourself to be a sinner before the holy God, repented of your sins, trusted in Him as Savior, and turned to Him as Lord. Why is it important for you to continue to renew your relationship with Him through repentance?

4. How can you keep from taking prayer for granted and forgetting what a privilege it is that Christ opened a way for us to continually converse with our heavenly Father?

5. How can implementing prayer in decision-making processes prevent fear of making a mistake and paralysis?

6. Think about the truth that you pray to the Father through the Son by the power of the Holy Spirit. What does this mean? Why is it comforting that we don't have to climb a ladder to talk with God, but that Jesus is the ladder who bridges the gap between sinners and a holy God?

7. What are you praying for and wondering if God has heard? While it should be comforting to Christians that God listened to Rachel, how would you caution a friend who views this story as a blanket promise that God has heard her request and will answer in the way she desires?

8. It's hard to pray for people over long periods of time when we see little change in their lives. For whom do you need to prevail in prayer? Or maybe you need to prevail in prayer because of your sin. If so, repent and by God's help return, observing His mercy and justice, and waiting continually on Him (see Hos. 12:6).

9. How does Romans 8:26–27 comfort you in your prayer life?

10. In light of what you've learned in this chapter, write out a prayer to God.

11. Seek to memorize Colossians 2:2–3 and use it in prayer.

4

The God Who Remembers

From the Patriarchs to Moses

Father, I won't go if You won't go before me, beside me, and behind me. I was on my knees again, praying about another speaking engagement. I had prepared well on paper and had practiced speaking to the walls in my study, but I knew that no amount of preparation would bring about fruitfulness if the Spirit of God didn't do a mighty work in my heart and my listeners' hearts. And so I pleaded with the Lord to take over and transform hearts and minds. It's a prayer I find myself praying repeatedly before I speak at events or teach a Bible study. I'm deeply aware of my dependence on the Spirit to do anything for Jesus. My prayer isn't unlike Moses's prayer in the book of Exodus. He had been commissioned to lead the people to Canaan, but he wouldn't go unless the Lord went with them (Ex. 33:15). We're going to take a look at a few of Moses's prayers in this chapter, but first let's consider where we are in the storyline of Scripture.

Providential Pity

As we study prayer through the lens of biblical theology, we're learning more about the Bible. We began our study in Genesis in the account of creation and the fall. Next we looked at how the narrative of the flood shapes our prayers. In the last chapter we looked at the patriarchal period. Now we come to the Mosaic period, which begins in the book of Exodus.

After Israel settled in Goshen (Gen. 47:1–12), it wasn't long before the seventy descendants of Jacob increased greatly and multiplied, until the people of Israel were a strong force in Egypt (Ex. 1:1–7). The new king over Egypt had not known Joseph, and he greatly oppressed Israel. During this time a baby boy was born to a Levite couple. Since the king of Egypt had ordered all of the male Hebrew babies to be killed, this courageous couple hid him for three months and then put him in a basket among the reeds by the bank of the river (2:3). Moses purposefully uses the same Hebrew word for this basket that he had used for Noah's ark. The Lord brought both Noah and Moses through water to safety, preserving the godly line.

While bathing, Pharaoh's daughter found the basket and had pity on the crying baby boy. This was a providential pity! She didn't know that the baby's older sister, Miriam, was watching from a distance. Miriam asked Pharaoh's daughter if she would like for her to find a Hebrew woman to nurse him. When she said yes, Miriam got the baby's mother, Jochebed. When Jochebed appeared before Pharaoh's daughter, she received her son back in her arms. Only after he was weaned did she return him to Pharaoh's daughter to be raised as her son. Pharaoh's daughter named him Moses, and he grew up among Pharaoh's household, receiving an Egyptian education and training (Ex. 2:4–10).

In God's providence He put this baby boy in just the right place at the right time, orchestrating all the events in order for him to become part of Pharaoh's household. What appears to be a tragic story (What mother can stand to part with her baby boy or young son?) is a triumphant story of God's power and grace. This baby boy would grow up to be Israel's deliverer, foreshadowing the greater deliverer to come, Jesus Christ.

If you're questioning God's providence right now, this story invites you to bow your head and pray, trusting in God's goodness and sovereignty. Oftentimes we can't understand His ways, but we can trust Him. What seems to be tragic is turned to good in our Father's hands (Gen. 50:20).

Don't Argue with God

In the meantime, the Israelites were groaning under the yoke of slavery and cried out for rescue, "and their cry came up to God because of the bondage. So God heard their groaning, and God remembered His covenant with Abraham, with Isaac, and with Jacob. And God looked upon the children of Israel, and God acknowledged them" (Ex. 2:23–25). The word "remembered" in Scripture can be easily glossed over, but it's significant. God always remembers His promises. When He hung the bow in the clouds as a sign of the Noahic covenant, He said, "It shall be, when I bring a cloud over the earth, that the rainbow shall be seen in the cloud; and *I will remember* My covenant which is between Me and you and every living creature of all flesh" (Gen. 9:14–15). The sign was for both God and His people. We pray to the God who remembers and keeps His promises. Pray them back to Him in prayer. He always makes good on His word.

Because He remembered His covenant with the patriarchs, the Lord would use Moses to deliver His people from the oppressive yoke of Pharaoh. Just as He had initiated a relationship with Adam, Noah, Abraham, Isaac, and Jacob, He initiated a relationship with Moses. He called to him from a burning bush on Horeb, the mountain of God (also known as Mount Sinai), and Moses responded, "Here I am" (Ex. 3:4). God told Moses to remove his sandals to show that he was standing on holy ground, and then He revealed Himself as the God of Abraham, Isaac, and Jacob. Moses was afraid of God and hid his face (v. 6). But the Lord continued speaking: "I have surely seen the oppression of My people who are in Egypt, and have heard their cry because of their taskmasters, for I know their sorrows. So I have come down to deliver them out of the hand of the Egyptians, and to bring them up from that land to [Canaan]" (vv. 7–8).

He called Moses to bring His people out of oppression. But Moses didn't think the Lord had the right person because he didn't have confidence that he could accomplish God's calling. The Lord promised His presence and a sign: "I will certainly be with you. And this shall be a sign to you that I have sent you: When you have brought the people out of Egypt, you shall serve God on this mountain" (Ex. 3:12).

Moses wasn't finished speaking with God. He was unsure of his task. So he asked Him what he should tell the people if they asked, "What is the name of the God of our fathers?"

God replied, "I AM WHO I AM" (Ex. 3:14); and, "The LORD God of your fathers, the God of Abraham, the God of Isaac, and the God of Jacob, has sent me to you." He told Moses, "This is My name forever, and this is My memorial to all generations" (v. 15). In other words, the Lord is His covenant name. This is the God who condescended to His people by way of covenant. Jesus would use this language in His "I am" statements (see John 6:20, 35, 48, 51; 8:12, 24, 28, 58; 9:5; 10:7, 9, 11, 14; 11:25; 14:6; 15:1; 18:5).

The Lord told Moses just what He should say to the Israelites. He promised to deliver them out of Egypt and lead them into Canaan. Although Pharaoh would not willingly let them go, the Lord would display His power over the so-called gods of the Egyptians. And in the end, the Israelites would plunder them. But Moses still wasn't confident the people would believe him. So the Lord gave him powerful signs he could perform if the people didn't listen. Still, Moses was filled with unbelief. This time he used the excuse of being ineloquent. So the Lord promised His presence, "Now therefore, go, and I will be with your mouth and teach you what you shall say" (Ex. 4:12). But still Moses asked Him to send someone else (v. 13). This time the Lord's anger burned against Moses. Yet in His mercy, He gave Moses another mouth—that of his brother, Aaron. Moses would lead and Aaron would speak. They would work as a team.

This conversation between the Lord and Moses anticipates the events that unfold in the exodus from Egypt, but it's also the beginning of Moses's prayer life (Ex. 5:22–23; 6:12; 8:12, 30; 9:33). The climactic moment comes when Moses and the Israelites sing to the Lord with grateful hearts for His deliverance (15:1–18). The Lord had triumphed gloriously over Egypt's gods and king. He had displayed His power and holiness, His steadfast love and faithfulness. The Lord is King!

There are times when the Lord asks us to do something difficult. Perhaps you have a class full of wiggly first graders, most of them boys, and you think you won't be able to survive the year. You want another teacher to take over. Or maybe graduate school is too hard. You're drowning in papers and you wonder if you're the right person to be pursuing this degree. Perhaps one of your children has special needs, and you don't feel adequate to take care of him. You wonder if the Lord knew what He was doing when He called you to care for your dear child. Maybe you are married to a man who is far different from you and it's made some things difficult, yet you know you're called to love and serve him. You catch yourself wondering if the Lord got it right when He put the two of you together. Go to the Lord in prayer. Talk to Him about your feelings of inadequacy and deficiency, but don't argue with His plan. Trust that you are the right teacher for that class, that you can depend on Him to get you through graduate school, that you are the right mother for your child and the right wife for your husband. There are no mistakes with the Lord. Ask Him to help you see your circumstances with eyes of faith. And thank Him for what He is doing in your heart through the challenges.

We Don't Have to Be Afraid of God

After a difficult journey that lasted about seven weeks, Israel finally arrived at Mount Sinai.[1] While Moses went up the mountain to God, the people camped around it. This was in fulfillment of the sign God told Moses He would give him (Ex. 3:12). At Sinai the Lord made a covenant with all Israel through the covenant mediator Moses. The sum and substance of this covenant is found in the Ten Commandments (34:28). The people could not talk to God on top of the mountain because they were not consecrated. The holiness of God could not dwell in their midst. Yet in the thunder and flashes of lightning and the sound of the trumpet and the mountains smoking,

---

1. *ESV Study Bible*, note on Exodus 19:1–3 (Wheaton, Ill.: Crossway Bibles, 2008), 174.

the Lord talked with them from heaven (20:18). But they didn't want to speak to God because they were terrified of Him: "Then they said to Moses, 'You speak with us, and we will hear; but let not God speak with us, lest we die'" (v. 19). Have you ever felt that way? In the wake of sin and shame, it's easy to be terrified to talk to God. Sometimes we wonder if He will forgive us. Other times we're so filled with shame we can't bring ourselves to tell Him what we've done. We might be willing to talk with a Christian counselor, a sister in Christ, or maybe even a pastor, but not with God.

The author of Hebrews alludes to this story, saying to his congregation,

> For you have not come to the mountain that may be touched and that burned with fire, and to blackness and darkness and tempest....
> You have come to Mount Zion and to the city of the living God, the heavenly Jerusalem, to an innumerable company of angels, to the general assembly and church of the firstborn who are registered in heaven, to God the Judge of all, to the spirits of just men made perfect, to Jesus the Mediator of the new covenant, and to the blood of sprinkling that speaks better things than that of Abel. (Heb. 12:18, 22–24)

How glorious! We don't have to be afraid to speak with God. Yes, He is holy. Yes, we have every reason to be terrified of the Judge of all. But because the greater Mediator than Moses, Jesus Christ, has inaugurated the new covenant through His death on the cross, we can speak to God in confidence instead of cowardice, in joy instead of jitters, in festivity instead of fear. In your sin and shame, don't run away from Him; run to Him. He is the only safe place to go with your sin in order to confess it and repent of it.

We Can Intercede, but We Can't Save

After Israel confirmed the covenant they had made with the Lord to obey all He had commanded them to do (Ex. 24:1–8), the Lord called Moses to come up the mountain. There He would give him the tablets of stone on which He had written the commandments, and He would give instructions for building the tabernacle. One of the three items Moses was to include in the tabernacle is noteworthy for our study on prayer. The altar of incense was located in the Holy Place (Ex. 30:1–5; 37:25–29). The incense stood for the prayers of God's people. The altar's placement nearest to the curtain before the Most Holy Place signifies that prayer comes "nearest to the heart of God," and since "the offering was of a perpetual character," it reminds us of how much the Lord delights in the continual prayers of His people.[2]

We also learn some important things about prayer from the incident of the golden calf. While Moses was gone for forty days and nights, the people grew impatient waiting for their leader. They asked Aaron to make them gods that would lead them: "Come, make us gods that shall go before us; for as for this Moses, the man who brought us up out of the land of Egypt, we do not know what has become of him" (Ex. 32:1). Surprisingly, Aaron went along with their request and made a golden calf for them to worship (vv. 2–6). When the Lord told Moses what the people had done, He also told him that He was going to consume them in wrath so that He could make a great nation out of Moses: "I have seen this people, and indeed it is a stiff-necked people! Now therefore, let Me alone, that My wrath may burn hot against them and I may consume them. And I will make of you a great nation" (vv. 9–10). Moses implored the Lord not to do this. He questioned why His wrath burned against His people whom He had delivered. He was jealous for the Lord's reputation, not wanting the Egyptians to mock Him for delivering His people, only to consume them. Moses asked Him to turn from His anger and remember the covenant He made with His servants Abraham, Isaac, and Jacob (vv. 11–13). Amazingly, the Lord listened to Moses's imploratory and intercessory prayer, and He relented from consuming them. Does prayer matter? Yes! Our prayers are one of the means God uses to accomplish His sovereign plans.

---

2. Vos, *Biblical Theology*, 151.

After Moses confronted the people with their sin, he went up to the Lord to see if he could make atonement for it. He asked the Lord to either forgive them or blot him out of the Book of Life. In other words, he offered his life for theirs. But the Lord would not accept Moses as a sacrifice; He sent a plague on the people because of their idolatry (Ex. 32:30–35). Moses's request was denied because dying for the people was reserved for God's Son. Only Jesus, the sinless One, could offer His life for the forgiveness of the sins of God's people. His atoning sacrifice on the cross was the only one that could bring forgiveness of sins. He was the perfect substitute; Moses was not. We can intercede for others, but we can't save them. This is why we plead for the Lord to open people's eyes and bring them to repentance, that they may believe in the name of the Lord Jesus Christ, the only One who secures our place in the Book of Life (Ex. 32:33; Rev. 20:15).

We Won't Go If You Won't Go

When the Lord told Moses to depart from Mount Sinai with the people to enter the land of Canaan, He said that He would send an angel before them but would not go with them because they were a stiff-necked people (Ex. 33:1–3). But Moses would not go, not without the Lord. Outside the camp of the Israelites, he had pitched a tent of meeting. There the Lord "spoke to Moses face to face, as a man speaks to his friend" (v. 11). In that tent Moses interceded for the people. He asked the Lord not to send them to Canaan if He wasn't going with them. What was the point of going without Him? It was God's presence that distinguished them from every other people on earth (vv. 15–16).

Moses found favor in the Lord's sight, and he asked the Lord to show him His ways so that he could know Him. He also asked to see His glory. The Lord agreed to make all His goodness pass before him, proclaim His covenant name before him, and promise His grace and mercy, but He would not show Moses His face. So when Moses went up on Mount Sinai to receive the second set of tablets (he had broken the first two in anger over the golden calf), the Lord descended in the cloud, stood with Moses on the mountain, passed before him, and proclaimed, "The LORD, the LORD God, merciful and gracious, longsuffering, and abounding in goodness and truth" (Ex. 34:6).

In response, Moses bowed his head in worship and prayed, "If now I have found grace in Your sight, O Lord, let my Lord, I pray, go among us, even though we are a stiff-necked people; and pardon our iniquity and our sin, and take us as Your inheritance" (v. 9). No wonder Moses's face shone when he came down from the mountain; he had been talking with God (v. 29)!

In writing about our beloved Lord and Savior Jesus Christ, the apostle John recalls this conversation between God and Moses: "And the Word became flesh and dwelt among us, and we beheld His glory, the glory as of the only begotten of the Father, full of grace and truth" (John 1:14). No longer is it only Moses who was privileged to see God's glory. Jesus has come to show His glory! We have now seen God's face in Christ. In Christ we also, when we heard the gospel and believed in Him, were sealed with the Holy Spirit, who is the guarantee of our inheritance until God redeems His possession (Eph. 1:14). Think of it—we are God's inheritance! The glory of the Lord that filled the tabernacle anticipated the day when God's glory would come and tabernacle among us (Ex. 40:34; John 1:14). We don't have to go outside the camp to the tent of meeting to pray to God the Father. Jesus is the tent in which we pray to the Father by the Spirit. How glorious!

Moses's prayer that he would know the Lord in order to find grace in His sight is echoed by the apostle Paul in his prayer for the church in Colossae "that you may be filled with the knowledge of His will in all spiritual wisdom and spiritual understanding; that you may walk worthy of the Lord, fully pleasing Him, being fruitful in every good work and increasing in the knowledge of God" (Col. 1:9–10). This should be our prayer for ourselves, as well as for our families and church families, that we may know the Lord. One day we will know Him and His glory fully: "The city had no need of the sun or of the moon to shine in it, for the glory of God illuminated it. The Lamb is its light" (Rev. 21:23). Amazingly, God's people will also bring glory into the New Jerusalem: "And the nations of those who are saved shall walk in its light, and the kings of the earth bring their glory and honor into it" (v. 24). God's glory is reflected in His people made in His image. Only those whose names are written in the Book of Life will enter the gates of the city to "bring the glory and the honor of the nations into it" (v. 26).

Fiery Serpents and the Bronze Serpent

The tabernacle that Moses erected was a progression in God's dealings with His people in redemptive history. Although it may not seem as intimate as the Lord speaking with Abraham, Isaac, and Jacob, it must be remembered that His communication with the patriarchs was sporadic instead of bound up with a sacrificial system at the tabernacle in which prayer was offered regularly. The tabernacle was a symbol of God's presence in the midst of His people. The altar of incense, which stood outside the Most Holy Place, was a reminder that God delighted in the prayers of His people. Since Israel was traveling toward Canaan, they couldn't build a permanent structure yet. That would come in the days of David's son Solomon. Nevertheless, the tabernacle gave them a place to worship God throughout the wilderness journeys.

The book of Numbers catalogs these travels. Unfortunately, the people were characterized by grumbling instead of gratefulness, doubt instead of delight, lust instead of love, jealousy instead of joy, criticism instead of kindness, failure instead of faithfulness, and sin instead of self-control. During one of their episodes of impatience, the people spoke against God and Moses: "Why have you brought us up out of Egypt to die in the wilderness? For there is no food and no water, and our soul loathes this worthless bread" (Num. 21:5). Because of their sinful attitude and accusation, the Lord sent fiery serpents among them, which bit the Israelites and caused many of them to die (v. 6). Those who were still alive confessed their sin to Moses and asked him to pray to the Lord, asking Him to take the fiery serpents away. So Moses prayed on behalf of the people, and the Lord told him to make a fiery serpent to set on a pole so that everyone who was bitten could look at it and live (vv. 7–10).

The covenant of grace was administered differently in the Old Testament than in the New. Besides "promises, prophecies, sacrifices, circumcision, [and] the paschal lamb," there were "other types and ordinances delivered to the people of the Jews, all foresignifying Christ to come, which were, for that time, sufficient and efficacious, through the operation of the Spirit, to instruct and build up the elect in faith in the promised Messiah, by whom they had full remission of sins, and eternal salvation."[3] As the Israelites' eyes looked to the bronze serpent, the Lord God was giving them a picture of the cross of Christ. Sadly, the bronze serpent eventually became an object of idolatry for Israel and was destroyed under Hezekiah's reform (see 2 Kings 18:4).

Jesus refers to the story of the bronze serpent in the wilderness in His conversation with Nicodemus, a Pharisee and ruler of the Jews: "No one has ascended to heaven but He who came down from heaven, that is, the Son of Man who is in heaven. And as Moses lifted up the serpent in the wilderness, even so must the Son of Man be lifted up, that whoever believes in Him should not perish but have eternal life" (John 3:13–15). When you and I sin, we don't have to approach God through Moses or lift our eyes to a bronze serpent. We approach God through a far greater intercessor, Jesus Christ, and lift our eyes to the cross on which He accomplished our redemption. He has borne the penalty for our sins so that we can have eternal life in Him.

* * * * *

Can you relate to my prayer—*Father, I won't go if You won't go before me, beside me, and behind me*? Are you deeply aware of your dependence on the Spirit to do anything for Jesus? Perhaps you feel like Moses, commissioned to do a job you don't feel equipped to do. Remember that the Lord is with you. Talk to Him about your anxieties and fears, your feelings of inadequacy and loneliness. Don't run away from Him or the job He has called you to do. Run to Him and rest in His sustaining grace.

---

3. Westminster Confession of Faith 7.5.

Time to Ponder and Pray

1. In what present circumstances should you remember your need for the Spirit's help in order to glorify God? How will you pray during these times?

2. In what situation are you questioning God's providence right now? What do you know about the Lord and His promises that encourages you? How will you pray in light of this truth?

3. What has the Lord asked you to do that you find too difficult? What can you learn from Moses's feelings of inadequacy that will help you face your challenges? Have you thanked God for what He is doing in your heart through the challenges? If not, spend time doing so now.

4. What do you think about prayer? Describe a time when you have questioned if your prayers matter. What would you tell a friend who asked you why she should pray?

5. Whom do you need to intercede for? Spend time pleading with the Lord to open that person's eyes and bring him or her to repentance, that he or she may believe in the name of the Lord Jesus Christ, the only One who secures our place in the Book of Life.

6. Oftentimes we think that we have to clean ourselves up before we approach God. What is the implication for you that Moses requested God's presence *because* the Israelites were a stiff-necked people? In what area(s) do you need to ask forgiveness of sin? As you pray, what does it mean that the Lord has taken believers to be His inheritance, and what is your response to that truth?

7. Explain the glorious truth that Jesus is the tent in which we pray to the Father by the Spirit and why this makes you want to pray.

8. Have you, dear reader, lifted your eyes to the cross on which Jesus accomplished redemption, repented of your sins, and run to Him as your Redeemer?

9. In light of what you've learned in this chapter, write out a prayer to God.

10. Seek to memorize Colossians 2:2–3 to use it in prayer.

5

The Lord God Who Hears

From Moses to David and Solomon

What is your deepest yearning right now? What do you go to bed and wake up craving? If someone asked you what one thing you most desired, what would you answer? You may be single and long to be married. Or you are married and yearn for a child. It may be that you are in a job you don't like and desire a different one. Your husband may not be the spiritual leader that you had hoped he would be, and you long to see him grow in godliness. Physical pain may be your constant companion and you desire the Lord to bring relief and healing. Your child may struggle in school, and you want to make things easier for him. A friend or family member may have walked away from Christ and the church years ago, and you long for her to repent and return. Financial struggles may have taken their toll on your family, and you wish earnings would increase. A child's choices may awaken you in the middle of the night, and you long for her to see her sin and her need for a Savior. A troubled marriage, either your own or that of someone close to you, may weigh on your mind, and you yearn for things to be better. Caring for your aging parents has been a lot for you to handle, and you desire help from others who will serve them well, yet finances always seem to be an obstacle.

What do we do with our good desires when they seem to go unfulfilled day after day, month after month, or year after year? Is there anyone who cares? Anyone who hears? Anyone who can actually do something about them?

Long ago there was a woman who desired to have children but had not been able to get pregnant. She took her longing to the Lord in prayer and poured out her heart before Him. He heard her cries and answered her. We pray to the Lord God who hears.

Hannah's Heartfelt Prayer

In the last chapter we left Israel in the wilderness, grumbling and complaining against Moses and ultimately against God. After Moses died the Lord raised up Joshua to lead the people into the Promised Land, the place where God would dwell with His people in the temple. Up to this point in redemptive history, the garden of Eden and the tabernacle had been the places where the Lord had temporarily dwelled with His people. The entire book of Joshua centers on the entry into and conquest of Canaan, the Promised Land. But then Joshua died, and we learn in the book of Judges that the people failed to conquer the land (Judg. 1:27–36). Instead, they did what was right in their own eyes because there was no king in Israel. The books of Judges and Ruth anticipate the beginning of the monarchy in Israel with King Saul and King David. Instrumental in the development of the story is a boy named Samuel whom God would raise up to be the prophet who anointed both of these kings.

Samuel's story begins with his mother's prayers even before he was born. His mother, Hannah, had a godly husband who loved her very much, but she was deeply grieved because she was childless. As painful as it is to face infertility today, it was even more difficult in Hannah's day. Since the Lord had promised to bless the obedience of His people with the fruit of the womb and curse the disobedience of His people by withholding children (Deut. 28:4, 11, 18; see also Ps. 127:3), barrenness was often seen as a curse. Furthermore, a woman's status within her family was linked to motherhood. Finally, a woman was often ostracized from society if she was barren.[1]

---

1. John H. Walton, Victor H. Matthews, and Mark W. Chavalas, *The IVP Bible Background Commentary: Old Testament* (Downers Grove, Ill.: IVP Academic, 2000), 281.

But in her disappointment and distress, Hannah turned to the Lord in prayer instead of turning away from Him. Through prayer she had sought the Lord's presence in the house of the Lord in Shiloh. As she prayed, she made a vow to Him: "O LORD of hosts, if You will indeed look on the affliction of Your maidservant and remember me, and not forget Your maidservant, but will give Your maidservant a male child, then I will give him to the LORD all the days of his life, and no razor shall come upon his head" (1 Sam. 1:11). Hannah spoke to the Lord from the depths of her distress, praying from her heart. Her emotions ran so deep that Eli the priest even accused her of being drunk. But Hannah wasn't drunk at all. She was deeply troubled that she didn't have a child, so she pleaded with the Lord. Eli believed her when she told him she wasn't drunk and blessed her. Afterward, Hannah went on her way, ate some food, and was no longer sad.

In due time the Lord blessed Hannah with a son, and she named him Samuel, saying, "because I have asked for him from the LORD" (1 Sam. 1:20). After Hannah had weaned Samuel, she took him to the house of the Lord at Shiloh to Eli. She reminded him that she was the woman who had prayed in his presence years earlier and that here was the child the Lord had granted her. As hard as it must have been for Hannah, she kept her vow to give her son to the Lord.

Instead of regretting the vow she had made to the Lord and being bitter that she had to give up the son for whom she had waited so long, Hannah praised the Lord. Praise is the very heart of prayer:

> My heart rejoices in the LORD;
> My horn is exalted in the LORD.
> I smile at my enemies,
> Because I rejoice in Your salvation.
>
> No one is holy like the LORD,
> For there is none besides You,
> Nor is there any rock like our God....

For the pillars of the earth are the LORD's,
And He has set the world upon them.
He will guard the feet of His saints,
But the wicked shall be silent in darkness....

He will give strength to His king,
And exalt the horn of His anointed.
(1 Sam. 2:1–2, 8–10)

Encouragement from Hannah's Prayer

There are many treasures we can glean from Hannah's prayer life. Isn't it beautiful that the Lord invites His people to pour out their deepest disappointments and distress to Him? He hears and He answers. He granted Hannah a son. Out of His abundant grace, He later gave Hannah five other children, three boys and two girls (1 Sam. 2:21). We should not assume that this is a promise that God gives every barren woman children when she prays, but it's a reminder that He can do it, and if it's according to His plan and purposes, He will do it.

Significantly, prayer also changed Hannah. She was able to leave the house of the Lord and eat without being sad (1 Sam. 1:18). Our prayers don't change God's mind; they change us. Prayer is a means of grace that the Lord uses to align our will with His. We can pour out our hearts before Him knowing He hears us and will grant our request if it's according to His perfect will. Hannah's ability to eat without being sad revealed her trust in the Lord that was established through prayer.

Importantly, the heart of prayer is exultation. Hannah knew the Lord. She rejoiced in His salvation. She acknowledged His holiness and kingship. She extolled Him as Judge and Creator. And she sang about the Anointed One.

The Significance of Hannah's Prayer

Hannah's prayer is significant, opening the books of 1 and 2 Samuel, which close with David's song of deliverance (2 Sam. 22:1–23:7). This sets the stage for the next big event of redemptive history, a human king ruling over Israel in the land of Canaan. But its significance reaches much further than the historical books of 1 and 2 Samuel and 1 and 2 Kings. Mary reflects Hannah's prayer in her song about King Jesus in Luke 1:46–55:

> My souls magnifies the Lord,
> And my spirit has rejoiced in God my Savior....
> For He who is mighty has done great things for me,
> And holy is His name. (vv. 46–47, 49; cf. 1 Sam. 2:1–2)

Other passages in the New Testament draw from Hannah's prayer. Christ accomplished the salvation about which Hannah sang. He is the Rock that was with Israel in the wilderness (1 Cor. 10:4; cf. 1 Sam. 2:2). He "became for us wisdom from God" (1 Cor. 1:30; cf. 1 Sam. 2:3). He came as the Anointed One to bring good news to the poor and set at liberty the oppressed (Luke 4:18; 1 Sam. 2:4–8). God disarmed the evil rulers of this world, putting them to open shame by triumphing over them in Christ (Col. 2:15; 1 Sam. 2:9–10). He is

> Faithful and True, and in righteousness He judges and makes war.... And He has on His robe and on His thigh a name written:
> KING OF KINGS AND
> LORD OF LORDS. (Rev. 19:11, 16)

The adversaries of the Lord will be thrown into the lake of fire (20:15), but He will establish His throne in the New Jerusalem in which God Himself will dwell with His people (21:3).

The beauty of understanding that the Bible is one storyline with Christ as its center is that when we step back from the account of a woman's agony and anguish over infertility, her prayer, and her son who was given back to God, we see something far greater. Samuel was raised up by God to be a prophet in Israel to anoint the first two kings of Israel, who would point to the greatest and eternal King Jesus. Understanding the Bible this way invites us to see our smaller stories as part of the larger one.

The problem with most of our prayers is that they are too small. We forget to pray with God's kingdom purposes in mind. Often our prayers dwindle to our desires and disappointments. There's certainly nothing wrong with bringing our desires and disappointments to the Lord in honest prayer, but we need to pray with the whole story of Scripture in mind. When we do, our prayers change. The cries of a single woman turn from, "I want a man to spend my life with who will do this and that with me or for me" to, "Please grant me a man I can serve alongside for the sake of the gospel." The pleas of a mother with young children who seem out of control and chaotic turn from, "Grant me peace and quiet in this home" to, "Help me train these children in the ways of the Bible so that they can be a light for You." The prayers of a career woman turn from, "Help me make it through another day with this company" to, "Show me how I can use my gifts to bring you glory here, and give me opportunities to tell a coworker about the gospel today." The quiet cries of a woman caring for her aging parents go from, "Deliver me from this stress" to, "Help me display the kindness of Christ in all that I say and do."

A Man after God's Own Heart

As the story of Samuel moves forward, the Lord calls him to be a prophet to Israel (1 Sam. 3:1–4:1). After Samuel had grown old, Israel demanded that he appoint a king over them to judge them like all the other nations. In his displeasure over their request, Samuel prayed to the Lord, and the Lord told Samuel to give them what they demanded, a king to reign over them. They had rejected God, not Samuel. In His grace, the Lord told Samuel to warn them of the kind of king who would rule over them. But the people didn't heed his warning. They wanted to be like the nations around them with a king to judge them and fight their battles (8:4–9).

The Lord chose Israel's first king (1 Sam. 9:15–16). In the period of the judges, the Lord showed His people what chaos ensued when there was no king in Israel. In Saul the Lord would show His people what chaos ensued when there was a bad king in Israel. Instead of being a man after God's heart, Saul served his own selfish desires. He was a taker instead of a giver. Filled with anger and envy, jealousy and rivalry, he lost the kingdom because he disobeyed the Lord

(1 Sam. 13:13–14). Both Samuel and Saul prepared the way for Israel's second king, David, a man after God's own heart.

In 2 Samuel 7, God made a covenant with David concerning an eternal kingdom with an eternal Davidic king. First, God promised David a position, taking him from being the shepherd of sheep to a shepherd-king over His people. Second, God promised David a place. Israel would be planted in their own land. Third, God promised David peace. In their own place, Israel would have rest from their enemies. Finally, God promised David progeny. The Lord would raise up David's offspring and establish his kingdom forever.

In response to God's promises, King David prayed (2 Sam. 7:18–29). David began by responding to the Lord's covenant humbly: "Who am I, O Lord GOD? And what is my house, that You have brought me this far?" (v. 18). Humility must be the posture of all prayer. David didn't presume upon God's grace. Instead, he recognized that the Lord was orchestrating these great events in his life for His glory.

David also responded to the Lord's covenant by praising God's character: "Therefore You are great, O Lord GOD. For there is none like You, nor is there any God besides You, according to all that we have heard with our ears" (2 Sam. 7:22). Praise is the very heart of prayer. David's heart was filled with gratitude that he expressed in the worship of God's greatness.

Furthermore, David connected himself to God's covenant people: "And who is like Your people, like Israel, the one nation on the earth whom God went to redeem for Himself as a people…. For You have made Your people Israel Your very own people forever; and You, LORD, have become their God" (2 Sam. 7:23–24). This is the crux of the covenant of grace. It's the golden thread that runs through Scripture from Genesis through Revelation. He is our God, and we are His people. He will stop at nothing short of redemption and then the consummation of His kingdom.

Finally, in courage David asked God to confirm forever the promise He had spoken to David and to bless his progeny: "Now therefore, let it please You to bless the house of Your servant, that it may continue before You forever" (2 Sam. 7:29). David wasn't just concerned about his lifetime. He wanted God's blessing on his line. He wanted to know that God would bless his children and grand-children, his great-grandchildren and great-great-grandchildren.

A Superior King

David was not chosen for his greatness but so that he would point to the greatness of God's Son, Jesus Christ. Jesus is the son of David, the son of Abraham, the son of Noah, the son of Adam, the Son of God (Luke 3:31, 34, 36, 38). His kingship and kingdom are far superior to David's. His sacrifice on the cross makes possible the fulfillment of God's promise: "I will walk among you and be your God, and you shall be My people" (Lev. 26:12). He has reconciled us to God through the cross. In Christ the covenant of grace is eternally confirmed.

> But to the Son [God] says:
>
> "Your throne, O God, is forever and ever;
> A scepter of righteousness is the scepter of Your kingdom.
> You have loved righteousness and hated lawlessness;
> Therefore God, Your God, has anointed You
> With the oil of gladness more than Your companions."
> (Heb. 1:8–9)

As we pray we too need to humble ourselves before the Lord (James 4:10). We are more proud than we would like to admit. Some of us find it very difficult to depend on the Lord. Scripture repeatedly reminds us that we are weak against temptation and that pride is in all of our hearts. Dear friend, if you are arguing with the Lord about something in your life or arguing with someone else because you're not getting your way, please humble yourself before the Lord.

As we pray we also need to praise God's character. Oftentimes our list of petitions is so long that we spend far too little time acknowl-edging God's greatness. Try praising His character in alphabetical order: "I praise you, O Lord, for your awesomeness, beauty, creation, deliverance, eternality, faithfulness, greatness, holiness…"

In prayer it's also important not to forget that we are part of the covenant community. How often do you spend time in prayer for your pastors, elders, deacons, and the members of your church? Do you struggle in prayer on their behalf, asking God to show them His greatness in their lives? How often do you spend praying with other believers?

Finally, we need to pray David's prayer (2 Sam. 7:28), which is transformed on the lips of Jesus—"Sanctify them by Your truth. Your word is truth" (John 17:17)— for our children, grandchildren, and the covenant children in our churches. We need to pray that we will have opportunities to train the next generation in the ways of the Word and to be faithful in doing so.

His Mercy Is More

Even though God helped David carry out great military exploits and gave him the privileged position as king of Israel, David's life was far from perfect. David was guilty of both murder and adultery (2 Samuel 11). Yet in Psalm 51 David pleads with God in prayer. He begins with who God is:

> Have mercy upon me, O God,
> According to Your lovingkindness;
> According to the multitude of Your tender mercies. (v. 1)

Then he moves on to who he is—a sinner in desperate need of God's mercy:

> Wash me thoroughly from my iniquity....
> For I acknowledge my transgressions,
> And my sin is always before me.
> Against You, You only, have I sinned....
>
> Behold, I was brought forth in iniquity....
> Behold, You desire truth in the inward parts. (vv. 2–6)

He is aware of several things concerning his sinfulness. He is a sinner in the present. He has been a sinner since conception (what we would call original sin). And his sin is against God, the Judge of all the earth.

David is also aware of several things concerning God's mercy (Ps. 51:7–12). He acknowledges the Lord can cleanse him, and He mercifully does so with blood: "Wash me, and I shall be whiter than snow" (v. 7). David also recognizes that the Lord can create a new heart in him and keep him from falling away (vv. 10–11). Furthermore, David is confident that the Lord can restore to him the joy he had lost by wandering away from Him into sinful pastures (vv. 8, 12).

By God's grace David's sin led to a life of true worship by way of confession and God's cleansing. It also ended in witness and work (Ps. 51:13–19). David was able to teach others about God's mercy, holding out the hope of forgiveness. He did so primarily by worship: "O Lord, open my lips, and my mouth shall show forth Your praise" (v. 15). He also recognized the great need for God to work in the community of believers. In the wake of sin, David was well aware of the need for God to build the walls of Jerusalem, the place of the temple, and work in the hearts of the people so that there would not be empty worship or blatant sin: "Do good in Your good pleasure to Zion…. Then You shall be pleased with the sacrifices of righteousness" (vv. 18–19). Only as the Lord created hearts turned to Him in worship, hands for His work, and tongues for the witness of His name would Israel be a people that gave Him glory. The same is true for God's people today. Only as the Lord turns our hearts toward Him in worship, energizes our hands to be busy with His work, and empowers our lips to continually praise His name will we glorify and enjoy Him.

Sinners Need a Savior

David's prayer of confession reveals our sinfulness and our need of a merciful Savior. Jesus fully revealed the mercy of God when He came to earth (John 1:14). The perfect Lamb of God came to take away the sins of the world. We might be tempted to think sexual immorality, idolatry, adultery, homosexuality, and alcoholism are unpardonable sins, but Paul reminds us that Jesus forgives those once ensnared to these sins and gives them a new heart when they turn to Him in repentance and faith: "But you were washed, but you were sanctified, but you were justified in the name of the Lord Jesus and by the Spirit of our God" (1 Cor. 6:9–11). One of the questions our church asks people desiring church membership is whether they acknowledge that they are sinners in the sight of God. This is extremely important. Only when we recognize our sin do we realize our need for Jesus. But it is even more important to recognize the merciful Christ who purges us with His blood, washes us white as snow, blots out our sins with His blood, creates in us a clean heart by fulfilling the new covenant, dwells in us by His Spirit, and gives us His joy so that our joy may be full.

Jesus, the greatest High Priest, gave Himself as the final and perfect sacrifice that God did not despise. As the greatest Prophet, he also leads God's people in praise. And as the greatest King, He builds up the walls of the church, bringing in people from every tribe, tongue, and nation to cry glory to the Lamb. Both together and individually we must confess our sins to God and praise Him through prayer.

Solomon's Climactic Prayer

The period of the monarchy climaxed in David's son Solomon when he stated in his temple dedication prayer that the promises God made to David had been fulfilled (1 Kings 8:24). No longer would there be a tabernacle to set up and take down as there was in the wilderness. No longer would the ark of the covenant reside in the tabernacle in Shiloh (Josh. 18:1), Nob (1 Sam. 21:1), or Gibeon (1 Chron. 16:39).[2] Solomon brought it to the temple in Jerusalem, which he had built: "Then the priests brought in the ark of the covenant of the LORD to its place, into the inner sanctuary of the temple, to the Most Holy Place, under the wings of the cherubim" (1 Kings 8:6). And the young king blessed the Lord, acknowledging that God had fulfilled His promise

---

2. I. Howard Marshall, A. R. Millard, J. I. Packer, and D. J. Wiseman, eds., *New Bible Dictionary*, 3rd ed. (Downers Grove, Ill.: IVP Academic, 1996), 1145.

to David. Then Solomon stretched out his hands toward heaven and prayed (vv. 22–53).

Solomon prayed to the personal God who keeps His promises: "LORD God of Israel…who keep[s] Your covenant and mercy with Your servants" (1 Kings 8:23). The Lord God had condescended to His people by way of covenant. Solomon acknowledged God's greatness: "There is no God in heaven above or on earth below like You" (v. 23). He then based His prayer on God's promises: "Now keep what You promised Your servant David my father…. Let Your word come true" (vv. 25–26). Also, he acknowledged that although the temple is God's dwelling place, He cannot be contained to the highest heaven, much less to the temple Solomon had built (v. 27). Finally, he pleaded for God's judgment, forgiveness, or favor in specific situations. He asked that the Lord would listen to the prayers of His people that were made from within the temple or directed toward the temple and respond when He heard them. Notably, each of Solomon's seven requests has to do with sin, one of the great themes of the Bible. Throughout the storyline of Scripture we learn that we cannot solve the problem of sin ourselves. We need a solution to our sin, and that solution is found only in Jesus Christ, the One Solomon anticipates in his prayer.

First, Solomon asked the Lord to condemn the wicked and justify the righteous "when anyone sins against his neighbor" (1 Kings 8:31–32). His second, third, and fourth petitions were that God would forgive Israel when, facing defeat in battle, drought, or famine and pestilence, they acknowledged their sin and sought forgiveness (vv. 33–40). His fifth request was that when foreigners heard of God's greatness and prayed to Him, God would hear and respond for the sake of His great name (vv. 41–43). Sixth, he asked that the Lord would maintain Israel's causes in battle (vv. 44–45). In his final petition, Solomon anticipated that Israel would be exiled from the land because of sin; he asked that if they repented, the Lord would forgive them and grant them compassion (vv. 46–53).

The Great Progression

Do you see the progression? We began in the garden-temple with Adam and Eve enjoying perfect communion with God. Then after the fall, their communion with Him was broken, and they were forced out of the garden. In Seth's line people began to call on the name of the Lord, but wickedness filled the earth and the Lord judged humankind with the flood. Only Noah and his family were saved. The Lord initiated a relationship with Noah, making a covenant with him. In the patriarchal period, the Lord again initiated a relationship with Abraham, Isaac, and Jacob. Each of them prayed, and while their prayers were intimate, they were also sporadic. Moses was able to meet with the Lord in a small tent outside the camp, which was a step forward from the sporadic prayers of the patriarchs. He could go to the tent whenever he wanted to meet with God. Soon the tabernacle replaced Moses's tent, and it was superior because all Israel could pray there, not just Moses. After hundreds of years the tabernacle was replaced with the temple in Jerusalem. Now all nations—not just Israel—were welcome to pray toward the temple, calling on the name of the Lord, the King of the nations.

The Lord, speaking through the prophet Isaiah about two hundred years later, reminds His people of Solomon's words in indicting them for making His temple a place of idolatry and immorality:

> "Heaven is My throne,
> And earth is My footstool.
> Where is the house that you will build Me?
> And where is the place of My rest?
> For all those things My hand has made,
> And all those things exist,"
> Says the LORD.
> "But on this one I will look:
> On him who is poor and of a contrite spirit,
> And who trembles at My word." (Isa. 66:1–2)

Over seven hundred years after Isaiah began prophesying, the first martyr of the church, Stephen, repeated Isaiah's words in his speech when he indicted the Jews for being a stiff-necked people, those who betrayed and murdered the Just One (Acts 7:47–53). They had missed the whole point of the tabernacle and the temple, both of which pointed to Jesus, the Word who "became flesh and dwelt [tabernacled] among us" (John 1:14). Jesus is the true temple to whom we come to pray to the Father through the Son by the power of the Holy Spirit. In Christ we have forgiveness of sins. He welcomes both Jews and Gentiles, having torn down the barrier, making one new man through the cross (Eph. 2:14–16). Christ is building His church from every tribe, tongue, and nation (Rev. 7:9–10; 21:24–26). Believers are also temples because of the indwelling Holy Spirit (1 Cor. 3:16–17). We don't have to go to a certain location, such as Mount Gerizim in Samaria or Mount Moriah in Jerusalem (John 4:20). We have already come to Mount Zion, the city of the living God (Heb. 12:22–24). We can pray anywhere, anytime because we carry the temple around within us. How glorious!

Has someone wronged you? Take it to the Lord and let Him be the Judge. Are you feeling defeated because you once again raised your voice to your child, snapped at your husband, or binged and then purged? Turn again to the Lord in repentance, seeking His forgiveness. Does the paycheck look too little to pay the bills, the cancer diagnosis too big to handle? Take it to the Lord and ask Him to uphold you. All of us have sinned and fall short of the glory of God (Rom. 3:23). All of us have reason to plead in prayer for forgiveness. Take your sin to the Lord and cry out to Him to have compassion on you and forgive you. He is the great God who is faithful to keep His promises. You have every reason to believe He will hear your pleas and grant you compassion and forgiveness.

* * * * *

It's hard when you desire something so desperately and years go by without your desire being met. But you are not alone. Whether you desire an acceptance letter to your first choice of graduate schools, a husband, a child, or a better career, Hannah's story within God's larger story of redemption invites you to see your own story within it. Your pleas do not fall on deaf ears. Your tears do not fall to the ground unnoticed. The Lord God hears you. And He answers. It's not always in the way we want Him to answer. But His answers to our prayers are always good, wise, and gracious. When things don't go our way, we must trust that our heavenly Father's way is best. Then, regardless of the outcome, our hearts can exult in the Lord.

Time to Ponder and Pray

1. Describe a time when prayer changed you from experiencing deep distress to delighting in the Lord. How does this happen?

2. Hannah took Samuel to Eli and reminded him that she was the woman who had prayed years earlier and now was presenting her son. How do you make it a point to show and tell others of God's answers to prayers?

3. Is Hannah's story a blanket promise that we will get what we ask from the Lord? Why or why not?

4. Spend time exulting the Lord in your heart today, adapting Hannah's prayer in 1 Samuel 2:1–10 to your present circumstances.

5. Consider whether your prayers are too small, dwindling to your desires and disappointments. How will you change this if you need to?

6. How do your prayers reflect
   • humility?

   • praise of God's character?

   • petitions for your leaders, especially your pastors and elders?

   • petitions for the next generation to know the truth?

7. Is there a sin in your past, dear reader, that you think is separating you from God's love? Which of David's words in Psalm 51 comfort and convict you? How could you use this psalm to help a friend who doesn't believe God could ever forgive her for a specific sin?

8. What would you tell someone who asks you, "How can I know God will hear my prayers?"

9. In light of what you've learned in this chapter, write out a prayer to God.

10. Seek to memorize 1 Samuel 2:1–2.

6

The Lord Who Is Trustworthy

From Solomon to the Exile

Most of us reach a point in our lives when it seems as though our "glory days" have passed. We seem to have hit the height of our education, career, marriage, ministry, or parenting. We look back and mourn earlier days that were going so well and held great potential. If we're not careful, we get stuck in our past, thinking that the Lord is no longer with us, no longer using us, or no longer capable of doing powerful things in our midst. Anxiety and fear can rule in our hearts. It can appear that everything is against us—our age, health, season of life. We are plagued by disappointments and dashed dreams. We see problems more than we see the personal God who is with us in our problems. We get lost in our own stories, not sure where to turn or turning to all the wrong things instead of looking to God's story, which helps us navigate our days.

The glory days of Israel seemed to be in the past. Idolatry and immorality ruled the day. There were far more wicked kings than righteous ones. Yet the dawning light of the gospel continued to shine in Israel. Those who held fast to God's promises found Him to be trustworthy. You and I must constantly choose in whom or in what we are going to trust. Will it be our words and wisdom, or God's words and wisdom? We must plead with the Lord to help us because we will always choose our words and wisdom apart from His grace. We don't naturally listen to God. We don't naturally go to Him in prayer and pour out our anxious and fearful hearts. Yet we must. There is no help as great as the help of our God. There is no victory in anyone or anything else. There is no forgiveness apart from Him. There is no place for repentance and reform except at the feet of our Redeemer.

Have the Glory Days Passed?

In the last chapter we saw that the period of the monarchy climaxed in King Solomon, when the promises were fulfilled in Solomon's prayer of dedication (1 Kings 8:24). Sadly, it didn't take long—within Solomon's reign—for the monarchy to take a turn for the worse (1 Kings 11). Following Solomon's death, the country actually divided into the Northern Kingdom (Israel) and the Southern Kingdom (Judah) in 931 BC (1 Kings 12:16–24).

Elijah and Elisha preached to the Northern Kingdom during this time. Although there were a few good kings, the majority of kings in both Israel and Judah did evil in the sight of the Lord and led the people into rebellion. In His grace and mercy, God raised up prophets during this time to prophesy to the people of coming judgment so that they would turn and repent of their wicked ways. Hosea and Amos preached to the Northern Kingdom while Isaiah and Micah preached to the Southern Kingdom. Joel, Obadiah, and Jonah also preached their messages during this time. Tragically, the Northern Kingdom did not listen and was taken into captivity by the Assyrians in 722 BC.

A little over one hundred years later, the same thing happened to the Southern Kingdom, except it was the Babylonians who took them into captivity. This involved three different deportations in 605, 597, and 586 BC. In the second of these deportations, Jehoiachin, the last true Davidic king on the throne, was taken to Babylon along with the royal family and all the leading classes in Israel. God's promises seemed thwarted. The glory days seemed to be in the past. During this period of redemptive history, there were two prophets and two kings who lifted their voices to God in noteworthy prayers—Elijah and Elisha, and Hezekiah and Josiah.

Elijah's Prayer for the Widow's Son

We are first introduced to Elijah on the heels of reading about wicked King Ahab, who reigned over the Northern Kingdom in Israel for twenty-two years. His wife, Jezebel, the daughter of the king of the Sidonians, had led him into Baal worship: "Then he set up an altar for Baal in the temple of Baal, which he had built in Samaria. And Ahab made a wooden image [a Canaanite goddess]. Ahab did more to provoke the LORD God of Israel to anger than all the kings of Israel who were before him" (1 Kings 16:32–33). It was during this time that the Lord raised up Elijah to show His power over Baal, just as He had raised up Moses to show His power over the Egyptian gods. In preparation for this show of power, He ordained a drought over the land and eventually sent Elijah to confront King Ahab. During the drought, the Lord used Elijah to reveal His power in the life of a widow in Zarephath, a city on the coast of Phoenicia (1 Kings 17).

This widow had been ordained by God to feed Elijah. When Elijah saw her, he asked for a morsel of bread. But she had only a small amount of flour and oil, and she was about to prepare it for herself and her son so that they wouldn't die of starvation. Elijah encouraged her to do as she planned, but first he requested that she make him a little cake so he could have something to eat. At the same time, he gave her a promise from the Lord: "The bin of flour shall not be used up, nor shall the jar of oil run dry, until the day the LORD sends rain on the earth" (1 Kings 17:14). The widow did as Elijah asked, and the Lord's word proved true.

After this the widow's son became ill and died. The widow blamed Elijah: "What have I to do with you, O man of God? Have you come to me to bring my sin to remembrance, and to kill my son?" (1 Kings 17:18). But he asked her to give him her son, carried him to his own bed, and cried to the Lord, "O LORD my God, have You also brought tragedy on the widow with whom I lodge, by killing her son?… O LORD my God, I pray, let this child's soul come back to him" (vv. 20–21). When Elijah prayed, the Lord listened to him and revived the life of the child.

Notably, Elijah, a man of God, was outside the borders of Israel speaking with a Phoenician woman about the true God. Remember, God had promised Abraham that in him "all the families of the earth shall be blessed" (Gen. 12:3). Here is one example in the Old Testament of this promise coming to fruition. The widow in Zarephath confessed, "Now by this I know that you are a man of God, and that the word of the LORD in your mouth is the truth" (1 Kings 17:24).

Obviously Elijah was indebted to this woman for his food and lodging, and her accusation would have been upsetting. But Elijah knew where to go—to God in prayer. He used God's covenant name, Lord, and claimed Him as his God: "my God" (1 Kings 17:20). His question was not an accusation against the Lord as much as a cry of faith for the Lord to defend His name and display His power before this woman. He asked the Lord to revive her son's life, displaying His power over death, and He did.

This miracle of God raising the dead in the dark days of the Northern Kingdom, which were leading up to the exile at the hands of the Assyrians, anticipates another resurrection. We serve a God not of the dead, but of the living. Jesus raised Jairus's daughter and Lazarus from the dead to show His power over death (Matt. 9:18–23; John 11:1–44). Later He raised Himself from the grave to display this same power (see John 2:19–22; 10:17–18). He came to earth to conquer death so that He might set God's people free from it. Death could not hold our dear Lord and Savior in the grave, and it won't hold believers in the grave either. When Jesus returns He will resurrect our bodies, reuniting them with our souls so that we might stand in His presence in glorified (perfectly sanctified) bodies.

Are you accusing the Lord or one of His people for a hard providence in your life? The Lord who raised Himself from the dead sees you and hears your cries of distress. He will provide the faith that you lack right now. Seek His face, asking Him to strengthen your faith as He reveals His power to you through His word and works.

The Prayer of a Righteous Man

Certainly the private and prayerful confrontation of death at the widow's home prepared Elijah for the public confrontation of King Ahab, bolstering his confidence in the power of prayer. Elijah told King Ahab to gather all Israel to him at Mount Carmel along with the 450 prophets of Baal and the 400 prophets of Asherah (1 Kings 18:19). Elijah prepared a contest to show who was the true God, the Lord of Israel or Baal. Both the prophets of Baal and Elijah laid bulls on altars with no fire underneath them. Then the prophets were to call on the name of Baal and Elijah was to call on the name of the Lord, and whichever one answered by fire would prove to be God.

From morning until noon, the prophets of Baal tried to rouse their god to answer them and start a fire to prove he was god, but no Baal came to their aid. Finally it was Elijah's turn. He told the people of Israel to come near. He made trenches around the altar and ordered that four waterpots be poured over the offering, the wood, and into the trenches, obviously making burning an offering even more challenging. He prayed, "LORD God of Abraham, Isaac, and Israel, let it be known this day that You are God in Israel and I am Your servant, and that I have done all these things at Your word. Hear me, O LORD, hear me, that this people may know that You are the LORD God, and that You have turned their hearts back to You again" (1 Kings 18:36–37). And the Lord answered Elijah's prayer by letting His fire fall and consuming the burnt offering. "Now when all the people saw it, they fell on their faces; and they said, 'The LORD, He is God! The LORD, He is God!'" (v. 39).

The Lord used the prayer of a righteous man to bring about repentance in the hearts of His people. Elijah called on the covenant name of the Lord. And he set his prayer in the covenantal context of God's covenant with Abraham, which was reaffirmed with Isaac and Israel (Jacob). Elijah's concern was that the Lord's people recognize He alone is God. He longed for God's people to repent of their sinful ways and return to Him.

In the aftermath of this event, Elijah told Ahab to eat and drink because there was a sound of an abundance of rain (1 Kings 18:41). Elijah went to the top of Mount Carmel and bowed down, putting his face between his knees. He prayed for rain, and there was a great rain. The drought was over. The Lord had displayed His power and grace in answer to a prophet's prayer.

James refers to this story in his letter: "Elijah was a man with a nature like ours, and he prayed earnestly that it would not rain; and it did not rain on the land for three years and six months. And he prayed again, and the heaven gave rain, and the earth produced its fruit" (James 5:17–18). James used this story to highlight the importance of prayer: "The effective, fervent prayer of a righteous man avails much" (v. 16). We are to pray in every situation. When you are suffering, pray for God's healing. When you are cheerful, praise God for His blessings. When you are sick, ask the leaders of your church to pray for you. When you have sinned, pray for God's forgiveness. There is nothing too small or too great for which to pray. Our heavenly Father invites us to come to Him with everything on our hearts, anytime of day, anywhere we are. He delights to hear His children and display His power in our lives.

If God Is for Us, Who Can Be against Us?

The Lord took His prophet Elijah up to heaven by a whirlwind while Elisha, his successor, stood by and watched (2 Kings 2:11–12). Immediately before Elijah's departure from this earth, Elisha asked him for a double portion of his spirit to rest on him, and Elijah promised that his desire would be fulfilled if Elisha saw him being taken from him (vv. 9–10). Since Elisha saw Elijah being taken to heaven by a whirlwind with chariots of Israel and its horsemen, he began his ministry in Israel knowing that he had received a double portion of Elijah's God-given power.

Not long afterward, the king of Syria became a threat to Israel. Elisha sent word to the king of Israel on more than one occasion, warning him of the Syrians' locations in order to save him from harm. The king of Syria didn't suspect God's prophet was leaking their location, so he asked who among his own troops was a traitor. One of his servants clarified that it wasn't a traitor among his own troops, but the prophet of God, Elisha, who heard his plans and told the king of Israel (2 Kings 6:12). So the king of Syria sent a great army with horses and chariots to seize God's prophet.

Elisha's servant saw the army first and cried out in fear to Elisha, "What shall we do?" (2 Kings 6:15). Elisha replied in faith, "Do not fear, for those who are with us are more than those who are with them" (v. 16). Then Elisha went to God in prayer on behalf of his scared servant: "LORD, I pray, open his eyes that he may see" (v. 17). And the Lord opened the eyes of Elisha's servant so that he could see the horses and chariots of fire surrounding Elisha in order to protect him.

When the Syrians came toward him, Elisha prayed, "Strike this people, I pray, with blindness" (v. 18), and the Lord did. Then Elisha led them to the king of Israel. When they entered Samaria, he prayed, "LORD, open the eyes of these men, that they may see" (v. 20), and the Lord did so. The king of Israel could have easily struck them down and asked Elisha if he should kill the Syrians, but the prophet told the king not to kill them. Instead, he instructed him to set a feast before them before sending them back to the king of Syria, putting a stop to the Syrians' raids into Israel (vv. 21–23).

Sometimes when you're reading prayers in Scripture, praying seems so easy, doesn't it? Elisha prayed succinct, faith-filled prayers, and each one was granted exactly as he requested. Some people think God is like a genie in the sky, at their beck and call to deliver their sporadic and succinct requests. When He does, they are delighted; if He doesn't, they are distressed and often angry. We need to look closely at what is happening in this story to make sure we're drawing biblical conclusions about prayer.

Remember that Elisha was God's prophet for this time in redemptive history. He had been appointed to speak God's truth to the Northern Kingdom, especially since they were on a rebellious road leading to exile (2 Kings 17). In other words, Elisha was a man of faith and godliness, and his prayers were informed by God's words. In addition to this, notice that Elisha first prayed for his servant—not for himself or his enemy. He asked the Lord to bolster his servant's faith by opening his eyes to see the great spiritual army with which the Lord had surrounded Elisha. Only then did he pray for the Lord to strike his enemies with blindness so that he could lead them to King Jehoram in Samaria and end the matter peacefully, preserving his own life and ministry to Israel during this tumultuous time. Elisha's prayer, then, was never about his own preservation, but about the kingdom of God. He had work left to do in Israel before his death during Joash's reign (13:20). Furthermore, God's answers were about His larger plans and purposes in redemptive history. He can never be a personal genie for any of us because He doesn't serve at our beck and call. He is the master; we are His servants. Because Elisha's prayers were in accordance with God's will, He granted his requests.

Elisha's prayer for his servant is a beautiful one. We are often surrounded by people filled with fear. They see all of the opposition coming against them and none of the opportunities for God to display His mighty power. They don't know what to do in the face of unwanted suffering, unmet expectations, and unfulfilled dreams. They cry out in fear when the doctor tells them the terrible diagnosis, when the teenager admits to a sexual addiction, when the adult child leaves the church and condemns its teachings, when their marriage is troubled, and when the aging parent is diagnosed with dementia. We need to pray for the Lord to open their eyes to see that His power, protection, and provision are with them.

It's not just others who need this reminder. You and I need it too. The apostle Paul writes,

> If God is for us, who can be against us? He who did not spare His own Son, but delivered Him up for us all, how shall He not with Him also freely give us all things?… It is Christ who died, and furthermore is also risen, who is even at the right hand of God, who also makes intercession for us. Who shall separate us from the love of Christ? Shall tribulation, or distress, or persecution, or famine, or nakedness, or peril, or sword?…
>
> Yet in all these things we are more than conquerors through Him who loved us. (Rom. 8:31–32, 34–35, 37)

Who Will You Trust?

Several kings of Israel came and went, Elisha died, and the Northern Kingdom fell to the Assyrians in 722 BC. Because of their idolatry and immorality, Israel was exiled from their own land. Tragically, the Southern Kingdom (Judah) was following in Israel's footsteps. But it would be another 117 years before the first of three deportations to Babylon (605, 597, and 586 BC), where they too would face exile from the land at the hand of the Babylonians.

When Israel fell to Assyria, Hezekiah, king of Judah, was in the sixth year of his reign. King Hezekiah "trusted in the LORD God of Israel, so that after him was none like him among all the kings of Judah, nor who were before him. For he held fast to the LORD; he did not depart from following Him, but kept His commandments, which the LORD had commanded Moses" (2 Kings 18:5–6). Eight years later, in the fourteenth year of Hezekiah's reign, Sennacherib, king of Assyria, attacked Judah (v. 13). One of the Assyrian leaders implored Judah, "[Do not] let Hezekiah make you trust in the LORD, saying, 'The LORD will surely deliver us; this city shall not be given into the hand of the king of Assyria.' Do not listen to Hezekiah; for thus says the king of Assyria: 'Make peace with me by a present and come out to me'" (vv. 30–31).

You can hear the voice of the ancient serpent in the garden through the king of Assyria's words, can't you? Hezekiah could have given way to fear or fighting, but instead he went into the temple and sent a message to the prophet Isaiah, asking him to pray for the remnant in Judah (2 Kings 19:4). Isaiah sent an encouraging message back to Hezekiah, assuring him that the Lord would make the king of Assyria return to his own land and fall by the sword there (vv. 6–7). Upon reading Isaiah's message, Hezekiah spread it before the Lord and prayed (vv. 14–19).

In his prayer Hezekiah first acknowledged that he was praying to the covenant Lord: "O LORD God of Israel…You are God, You alone, of all the kingdoms of the earth. You have made heaven and earth" (2 Kings 19:15). This is where Jesus taught us to begin too: "Our Father in heaven, hallowed be Your name" (Matt. 6:9). Then Hezekiah asked,

"Incline Your ear, O LORD, and hear; open Your eyes, O LORD, and see" the situation he was facing with wicked Sennacherib, mocker of the living God and destroyer of the nations and their lands (2 Kings 19:16–18). Finally, Hezekiah asked the Lord to save them from Sennacherib's hand, "that all the kingdoms of the earth may know that You are the LORD God, You alone" (v. 19).

Hezekiah's prayer was answered because it was in line with God's holiness and justice, but most significant is the Lord's declaration: "For I will defend this city, to save it for My own sake and for My servant David's sake" (v. 34). That night the angel of the Lord killed 185,000 Assyrians, and after Sennacherib returned home to Assyria, his own sons killed him with a sword (vv. 35–37).

All those who are in the line of Christ, the true and final Davidic king, will be saved for the sake of God's great name. The salvation that the Father appointed has been accomplished in His Son. There came a day when instead of killing 185,000 in Jerusalem who were mocking the King of kings, the Father killed His own Son so that salvation would come to His people. When the world, the flesh, or the devil tempts you with the treats of this world, turn to the Lord you can trust, entreating Him in prayer to save you from anger or addiction, divisions or drunkenness, enmity or envy, idolatry or immorality, sensuality or strife. When your enemies taunt you in the midst of suffering to turn your back on God and stop trusting in Him, turn to Him, acknowledging that He alone can save. And when in the midst of service your enemies sow doubt that what you're doing for the Lord is accomplishing any good, turn to Him in faith, knowing that for the sake of His name and the name of His Son, He is using your efforts to bring forth gospel fruit.

Repentance in Prayer

After Hezekiah died, Manasseh became king for fifty-five years and then Amon for two, both of them doing what was evil in the Lord's eyes. During Manasseh's reign the Lord told Judah that He would give them into the hand of their enemies at a future point because of Manasseh's evil (2 Kings 21:10–15). But before exile came, one last good king assumed the throne in Judah, Josiah. King Josiah reigned for thirty-one years, doing what was right in the eyes of the Lord and walking in the ways of King David. He repaired the temple, during which time the Book of the Law was found. When Josiah heard the words of the Lord, his heart was penitent, he humbled himself before the Lord, tore his clothes and wept before the Lord, and the Lord heard him (22:19). Although the words of Josiah's prayer are not recorded, Scripture tells us that the Lord heard his prayer and promised that he would not have to see the disaster He was bringing on Jerusalem. Instead, he would die and be buried in peace before Jerusalem was destroyed (v. 20).

Josiah teaches us the posture of humility that is so important in prayer. He recognized that he and the inhabitants of Judah were sinners in need of God's grace. He acknowledged that the Lord's words had not been followed. He led the people in repentance, reforms, and restoring the Passover. Even so, the Lord did not turn away from His anger. Manasseh had provoked him, and He would cast off the city of Jerusalem that He had chosen and the temple of which He said, "My name shall be there" (2 Kings 23:27).

It's hard not to wonder how the Lord could ever forgive us when we look within our own hearts. That's true when we look inside our churches as well. But Jesus came to seek and to save sinners like you and me. When we are convicted of sin through God's word, we must repent. As James points out, "God resists the proud, but gives grace to the humble" (James 4:6). Like Josiah, we should "lament and mourn and weep! Let [our] laughter be turned to mourning and [our] joy to gloom. [We must] humble [ourselves] in the sight of the Lord, and He will lift [us] up" (James 4:9–10). Then we must trust in the Lord's forgiveness and rest in His grace: "If we confess our sins, He is faithful and just to forgive us our sins and to cleanse us from all unrighteousness" (1 John 1:9).

* * * * *

Perhaps you feel like the glory days have passed. You seem to have hit the height of your education, career, marriage, ministry, or parenting. You are looking back and mourning earlier days that were going so well and held great potential. Maybe you feel stuck, thinking the Lord is no longer with you, no longer using you, no longer capable of doing powerful things in your midst. Perhaps anxiety and fear rule your heart. Maybe you're focused on your disappointments and dashed dreams. Perhaps you're lost in your own story, not sure where to turn or turning to all the wrong things. During the days of the prophets Elijah and Elisha and the kings Hezekiah and Josiah, the dawning light of the gospel continued to shine in Israel. Those who held fast to God's promises found Him to be trustworthy. You and I will find the same. There is no help as great as the help of our God. There is no victory in anyone or anything else. There is no forgiveness apart from Him. There is no place for repentance and reform except at the feet of our Redeemer. Dear reader, run to Christ.

Time to Ponder and Pray

1. Describe a time when you felt the glory days were behind you in your education, career, marriage, or parenting. How did prayer help you through them?

2. Are you accusing the Lord or one of His people for a hard act of providence in your life? Remind yourself that the Lord who raised Himself from the dead sees you and hears your cries of distress. Also remember that He will provide the faith that you lack right now. How will you seek Him?

3. Make a list of the following:

   • people you know who are suffering, and pray for them

   • blessings the Lord has given you and others, and thank Him

- people you know who are sick, and pray for God's healing
- your sins, and ask for God's forgiveness

4. What would you tell a child who asks why God doesn't answer every prayer we pray in the way we want Him to answer it? How would you teach him or her that God is trustworthy?

5. What person do you need to pray for who is scared, asking God to open his or her eyes to see His power, protection, and provision?

6. In what situation is the enemy taunting you to turn your back on God and stop trusting Him? How will you turn toward Him instead?

7. Spend time confessing your present sins, asking God to forgive you.

8. When has it been hard for you to accept God's forgiveness for a specific sin? How would you encourage a friend who is having a hard time believing God could forgive her for something she has said or done?

9. In light of what you've learned in this chapter, write out a prayer to God.

10. Seek to memorize James 5:13–16.

7

The God Who Forgives

From the Exile to the Return to the Land

I have always taken great comfort in praying to my heavenly Father, knowing that I can take shelter under His almighty wings anytime, anywhere, about anything. There is great relief in coming before Him and submitting my will to His, praying in accordance with His word, and pouring out my heart in worship of His glory and grace. But I have not always understood prayer. At times I have wondered how my prayers make a difference. I have asked, *If God is sovereign and His plans are already decreed, what role do my prayers play?*

God's word makes it very clear that we are to pray and our prayers matter. Our prayers are a means that God uses to bring His purposes and plans to pass, and He has decreed them to be a part of His plan. Our prayers really do play a role in moving forward God's plan of redemption and restoration. They are a means that God graciously uses to accomplish His plan in this world.

God's servant and prophet Daniel knew that his prayers mattered. He knew that prayer linked him with heaven's throne room. He knew that his prayers were heard and were pleasing to the Lord's ears. He knew that when he prayed, God would hear and respond. How did Daniel know this? He knew this because he knew God's word: "If My people who are called by My name will humble themselves, and pray and seek My face, and turn from their wicked ways, then I will hear from heaven, and will forgive their sin and heal their land" (2 Chron. 7:14). Ezra, both a priest and a scribe skilled in the law of Moses, and Nehemiah, cupbearer to King Artaxerxes I, knew this too. And so in this chapter, we will look at the prayers of these three godly men whom God used to accomplish His plans and purposes.

God's Promises Seem Threatened

In the last chapter we learned about Josiah's prayer and reforms during his thirty-one-year reign in Judah. Even though Josiah walked in the ways of the Lord, exile was inevitable because of the wickedness of King Manasseh (2 Kings 21:10–15). After Josiah died in battle at the hand of Pharaoh Neco, king of Egypt, his son Jehoahaz became king. After three months Pharaoh Neco removed him from the throne and put another of Josiah's sons in his place, Jehoiakim, who reigned for eleven years. It was during Jehoiakim's reign that the Lord sent the Chaldeans (Babylonians), Syrians, Moabites, and Ammonites against Judah to destroy it because of Manasseh's sin (24:2–4).

After Jehoiakim died, his son Jehoiachin reigned in his place for three months. At that time Jerusalem was besieged by Babylon, and King Jehoiachin, the last, true Davidic king on the throne, gave himself up to the king of Babylon and was carried away. The king of Babylon then made Jehoiachin's uncle Zedekiah king, and he reigned for eleven years as the last king of Judah before it completely fell to Babylon in 586 BC.

In God's mercy He raised up both Daniel and Ezekiel to prophesy to the people during the exile. (Jeremiah was still prophesying during this time as well.) Daniel and Ezekiel spoke messages of both judgment and restoration to the exiles. God would still be faithful to His covenant promise; He would be their God, and they would be His people. Both Jeremiah and Ezekiel spoke of the promised new covenant, which Christ inaugurated during the last Passover that He celebrated with His disciples before His death (Jer. 31:31–34; Ezek. 37:21, 26; Luke 22:19–20).

The new covenant involved seven different promises. First, God promised His people would return to the land of promise. Second, God promised a restoration of the land. Third, God promised a realization of each of His previous promises to Adam, Noah, Abraham, Moses, and David. Fourth, God promised a renewed heart. Fifth, God promised the removal of sin. Sixth, God promised a reunion of Israel and Judah under one ruler, Jesus Christ. Finally, God promised the realization of redemption (this was the final covenant, and, as such, it secured redemption).

But during the exile and even during Ezra and Nehemiah's day, God's promises regarding the new covenant seemed threatened on every side. How did God's people display faith in prayer during these difficult days? We will first look at Daniel's prayer of confession.

Daniel's Prayer of Confession

Daniel was still living in Babylon when he prayed the prayer we read in Daniel 9:1–15. He had been in exile for many years. He was probably about eighty years old at the time of this prayer. In 539 BC Babylon fell to Persia, which was ruled by Cyrus. In 538 BC the first group of exiles returned to Jerusalem under Cyrus's decree. In 536 BC they began rebuilding the temple. From 536–530 BC they experienced much opposition to the rebuilding. Because of this opposition, the people completely stopped rebuilding the temple for ten years (530–520 BC). In 520 BC the rebuilding began again under Ezra's leadership, and the rebuilding of the temple was completed in 516 BC.

During Darius's first year (539 BC), Daniel, while reading Jeremiah's prophecy in Jeremiah 25:8–14 and 29:10–14, perceived that Israel would be in exile for seventy years. So he would have known that the seventy years were approaching their end:

> For thus says the LORD: After seventy years are completed at Babylon, I will visit you and perform My good word toward you, and cause you to return to this place. For I know the thoughts that I think toward you, says the LORD, thoughts of peace and not of evil, to give you a future and a hope. Then you will call upon Me and pray to Me, and I will listen to you. And you will seek Me and find Me, when you search for Me with all your heart. I will be found by you, says the LORD, and I will

> bring you back from your captivity; I will gather you from all the nations and from all the places where I have driven you, says the LORD, and I will bring you to the place from which I cause you to be carried away captive. (Jer. 29:10–14)

These words must have been like springs of water on a parched heart. God reminded Daniel of His promise to give His people a future and a hope. He reminded Daniel that His exile was not the final word and that it was almost finished. And He reminded Daniel to pray. So Daniel prayed.

Daniel turned his face to the Lord God in great humility, displayed by fasting, sackcloth, and ashes. When Solomon had finished the Lord's house and the king's house, the Lord appeared to Solomon and said to him, "I have heard your prayer, and have chosen this place for Myself as a house of sacrifice. When I shut up heaven and there is no rain, or command the locusts to devour the land, or send pestilence among My people, if My people who are called by My name will humble themselves, and pray and seek My face, and turn from their wicked ways, then I will hear from heaven, and will forgive their sin and heal their land" (2 Chron. 7:12–14). Although the temple of God did not exist in Babylon, God had not left His people. Though He had scattered them among the nations, He would be a sanctuary for them in the countries to which they had gone (Ezek. 11:16). Daniel remembered God's promise that He would hear from heaven, forgive their sin, and heal their land when His people cried out to Him in repentance and faith.

In his prayer Daniel first acknowledged who God is: "O Lord, great and awesome God, who keeps His covenant and mercy with those who love Him, and with those who keep His commandments" (Dan. 9:4). God's covenant is the reason behind His great love to redeem and restore a people for Himself through the work of His Son, Jesus Christ.

Second, Daniel confessed sin: "We have sinned and committed iniquity, we have done wickedly and rebelled" (v. 5). Notably, he includes himself among the people even though he has remained faithful to the Lord. He knows he too has sinned before a holy God.

He sees himself as a fellow struggler and sinner with the people of Judah. He admits their wickedness, rebellion, sin, wrongdoing, and turning away from His commandments.

Third, he confessed another sin: "Neither have we heeded Your servants the prophets, who spoke in Your name" (v. 6). The Lord had sent these prophets to speak to Israel's kings, princes, fathers, and to all the people of the land, but they had failed to listen to and heed their warnings. Instead, they indulged in idolatry and immorality.

Fourth, he contrasted people with God (vv. 7–10). God is righteous, but people are shameful because of their sin. The Lord is merciful and forgiving, but people are rebellious and disobedient.

Fifth, Daniel spoke of the beginning of the nation of Israel, when God gave the law of Moses and told His people about the blessings and curses of obedience or disobedience (vv. 11–14). He acknowledged God's faithfulness by bringing calamity on Israel, for this fulfilled His word. Yet Israel still did not repent and seek the Lord's face. They did not gain insight by God's truth.

Sixth, Daniel acknowledged the Lord's wonders and His people's wickedness: "And now, O Lord our God, who brought Your people out of the land of Egypt with a mighty hand, and made Yourself a name, as it is this day—we have sinned, we have done wickedly!" (v. 15). Both of these times of deliverance, from Egypt and from Babylon, point to the greater and final deliverance from the prince of this world, Satan, and his kingdom, which was inaugurated at Christ's first coming and will be consummated at His second coming.

Seventh, Daniel recognized that God's people were not fulfilling the role that the nation of Israel was supposed to play among the nations, "because for our sins, and for the iniquities of our fathers, Jerusalem and Your people are a reproach to all those around us" (v. 16). So he asked, "For the Lord's sake cause Your face to shine on Your sanctuary, which is desolate" (v. 17). They were to be a light to the nations, a kingdom of priests, and a holy people who would draw others to God (Ex. 19:6). But sadly, they were instead a byword among all those around them.

This is why they were sent into exile and dispersed among the nations. God's plan from the beginning was bigger than just the kingdom of Israel. But they didn't fulfill their commission to be a witness to the nations from within their land, so God sent them out of their land. And through faithful witnesses such as Daniel and his three friends, God's promise to Abraham that "in you all the families of the earth shall be blessed" (Gen. 12:3) was in part fulfilled in Babylon.

Because Israel was a byword among all those around them, Daniel pled that for His name's sake God would make His face to shine on the sanctuary in Jerusalem so that it would be rebuilt and the people could serve and worship God again according to His commands.

Finally, Daniel implored the Lord: "Incline Your ear and hear; open Your eyes and see our desolations" (Dan. 9:18). His prayer is based on God's mercy, "for we do not present our supplications before You because of our righteous deeds, but because of Your great mercies" (v. 18). He cried out for God's forgiveness, attention, and swift action for His name's sake: "O Lord, hear! O Lord, forgive! O Lord, listen and act! Do not delay for Your own sake, my God, for Your city and Your people are called by Your name" (v. 19).

How faithful God was to answer Daniel's prayer! Though a remnant did return and were able to worship God again, the true temple came when Christ became God in the flesh, dwelling (literally "tabernacling") among His people (John 1:14). God was moving forward His plan of redemption and restoration by showing His people that the physical temple pointed toward the presence of God, which came in Christ, the true temple. This is why John does not see a temple in his vision of the new heaven and the new earth in Revelation 21:22, because "the Lord God Almighty and the Lamb are its temple." The temple that was established in the garden of Eden with God's presence, the tabernacle that Israel set up in the wilderness and during the beginning years in Canaan, and the temple that Solomon built in Jerusalem all pointed to the final realization of the true temple, God's presence, in Jesus Christ.[1]

---

1. For a fuller discussion of this, see G. K. Beale, *The Temple and the Church's*

Great Guilt

Following the exile, God raised up the prophets Haggai, Zechariah, and Malachi to continue speaking to His people. Although the promises of God could not be completely fulfilled until Jesus Christ came, there was a partial fulfillment of a restored temple, people, and land under the leadership of Ezra and Nehemiah, whose ministries took place during the days of these prophets.

Between four and five months after Ezra arrived in Jerusalem, leading men of Israel informed him that the people had not separated themselves from the nations around them but had instead intermarried with them. The Lord had not only forbidden such intermarriages, but He had also warned Israel what would happen as a result of them (see Ex. 34:11–16; Deut. 7:1–11). Out of His love, the Lord chose to redeem Israel to be a people for His own possession, and as such He was jealous for their love. Intermarrying with those who worshiped other gods would be a snare for Israel that would bring judgment on them. Refraining from rebellion would result in Israel being a kingdom of priests and a holy nation for the Lord God. Tragically, we learn that just as Israel rebelled before the exile, the returned exiles (the first wave under King Cyrus) had also rebelled. Intermarriage was not an isolated problem but had occurred among the officials, the chief men, the priests, the Levites, and the people of Israel. Ezra's response to such rebellion was not a position of resignation but a repentant response. Ezra recognized that he was part of the covenant community and therefore was responsible to confess the sins of the people.

Ezra's prayer is instructive. Ezra began by expressing his shame and humiliation over sin: "O my God, I am too ashamed and humiliated to lift up my face to You, my God; for our iniquities have risen higher than our heads, and our guilt has grown up to the heavens" (Ezra 9:6). He understood the holiness of God and the rebelliousness of man. Then he recalled Israel's entire history of rebellion,

---

Mission: A Biblical Theology of the Dwelling Place of God (Downers Grove, Ill.: IVP Academic, 2004).

as well as the consequence of exile (v. 7). He recognized God's grace in leaving a remnant to repair the ruins of the temple and to return to being a people ruled by God's word (vv. 8–9). Finally, in verses 10 through 15, Ezra grieved that Israel had not responded to God's grace with thankful obedience but with faithlessness: "O LORD God of Israel, You are righteous, for we are left as a remnant, as it is this day. Here we are before You, in our guilt, though no one can stand before You because of this!" (v. 15).

Through his prayer, Ezra, the priest and intercessor for Israel, anticipates Jesus, the final and perfect priest and intercessor for the people of God. Jesus wept over the rebellious people in Jerusalem and longed for Israel to recognize the day of God's favor. Yet they would have none of it. Even so, by the time of the first chapter of Acts, there is a small remnant of about 120 believers. God's grace never fails; His plan of redemption will prevail. Peter says of God's people, "But you are a chosen generation, a royal priesthood, a holy nation, His own special people, that you may proclaim the praises of Him who called you out of darkness into His marvelous light; who once were not a people but are now the people of God, who had not obtained mercy but now have obtained mercy" (1 Peter 2:9–10).

Prayerful Preparation

About thirteen years after Ezra's arrival in Jerusalem under the reign of King Artaxerxes in 458 BC, the Lord raised up Nehemiah in 445 BC to rebuild the walls of Jerusalem. This also occurred under Artaxerxes, whom Nehemiah served as cupbearer, a prestigious position. Nehemiah learned from his brother that the returned exiles and the city were not doing well. The somber news pierced his heart in such a way that he wept and then continually fasted and prayed before the God of heaven, the only One who could make things right again. Nehemiah's prayer, recorded in Nehemiah 1:5–11, teaches us several aspects of prayer that should inform our own prayers to God.

Nehemiah's prayer begins with who God is: "I pray, LORD God of heaven, O great and awesome God, You who keep Your covenant

and mercy with those who love You and observe Your commandments" (Neh. 1:5).

Following this, Nehemiah recognized he was a sinner alongside
his kinsmen: "Both my father's house and I have sinned. We have
acted very corruptly against You" (vv. 6–7). He knew that he and his
family were just as guilty of sin as anyone else. He recognized that his
relationship with his kinsmen was covenantal, and so he prayed with
the pronoun "we" instead of "they."

Then Nehemiah recognized God's words and His works and
grounded his petition in both (vv. 8–10). He recalled the words of the
Lord through Moses promising restoration to the land after repentance, "but if you return to Me, and keep My commandments and
do them, though some of you were cast out to the farthest part of
the heavens, yet I will gather them from there, and bring them to the
place which I have chosen as a dwelling for My name" (v. 9). He also
remembered the work of the exodus, when the Lord delivered Israel
from Egypt through the Red Sea (v. 10).

Finally, he recognized that only God had the power to position him favorably before the king and give him success in regard to
his request (v. 11). This is a favor that the Lord granted Nehemiah
(2:5–8).

Nehemiah's prayer anticipates Christ, the Lord and Servant of
the covenant, who comes to deliver us from sin, death, and the devil
and make us new creatures with new hearts and new names. Because
of this great deliverance, Jesus has opened the way to the throne
room of grace again. And it is at the throne of grace that we find the
attentive ear of our Father, who is eager to grant us grace and mercy
because of the intercession of His Son. When we come before Him,
we need to acknowledge who He is (God Almighty), who we are
(sinners in need of grace), God's words and works, and God's power
to act. This puts us in a posture of humility and grounds our faith in
God's promises as we look to Him, trusting He will act in behalf of
His people.

A Prayer of Confession

Despite much opposition, Nehemiah had led the people in rebuilding the wall, a task that was now finished. After celebrating the Feast of Trumpets, the Day of Atonement, and the Feast of Booths, the people of Israel gathered together in order to confess their sin to the Lord and renew their covenant with Him. A quarter of the day was spent reading the law of Moses (the first five books of the Bible), and another quarter of the day was spent in confession and worship led by the Levites. There are several things we learn in this prayer of confession about God, His covenant with His people, and their response to His covenant (Neh. 9:6–38).

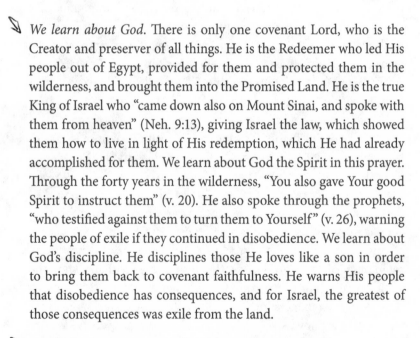

We learn about God. There is only one covenant Lord, who is the Creator and preserver of all things. He is the Redeemer who led His people out of Egypt, provided for them and protected them in the wilderness, and brought them into the Promised Land. He is the true King of Israel who "came down also on Mount Sinai, and spoke with them from heaven" (Neh. 9:13), giving Israel the law, which showed them how to live in light of His redemption, which He had already accomplished for them. We learn about God the Spirit in this prayer. Through the forty years in the wilderness, "You also gave Your good Spirit to instruct them" (v. 20). He also spoke through the prophets, "who testified against them to turn them to Yourself" (v. 26), warning the people of exile if they continued in disobedience. We learn about God's discipline. He disciplines those He loves like a son in order to bring them back to covenant faithfulness. He warns His people that disobedience has consequences, and for Israel, the greatest of those consequences was exile from the land.

We learn about God's covenant. Out of His love and grace, God chose Abraham to be one of His special people and delivered him out of the pagan land of Ur. God "found his heart faithful...and made a covenant with him" (Neh. 9:8). He promised Abraham four things—His presence, a special people, a possession (the Promised Land), and a purpose (the King of kings would come through his line). Since the

Lord is righteous in all He does, He keeps His promises perfectly: "You have performed Your words, for You are righteous" (v. 8). This is why He can be forgiving, gracious, and merciful; slow to anger; abounding in steadfast love; and never forsake His people even when they break covenant with Him. His covenant is not based on His people's performance, but on His promises.

We learn about Israel's response to God's covenant:

> They were disobedient
> And rebelled against You,
> Cast Your law behind their backs. (v. 26)

They were presumptuous, stubborn, and disobedient to God's commands. They failed to consider His wonders and wanted to return to Egypt. They were impatient, fashioning idols to worship instead of worshiping God in the way He had prescribed. At times things seemed to be going well. God's people would obey for a while, especially during the days of Joshua, but then during the time of the judges everyone did what was right in their own eyes because they ignored the true King of Israel. They were murderers of God's prophets and blasphemers, working evil until their suffering was so severe that they cried out to God, and He would send deliverers to save them from their enemies. But this would not last:

> After they had rest,
> They again did evil before You.
> Therefore You left them in the hand of their enemies. (v. 28)

So the cycle continued on and on throughout Israel's history until they experienced the curse of exile.

In light of these three things, Ezra and Nehemiah's generation came humbly before the Lord. They recognized Him as the great and awesome covenant-keeping God. They realized they stood before Him as covenant breakers, along with the generations before them. And they renewed their covenant commitment to Him as a new generation of those who have heard the law of God and want to commit themselves to obeying it.

As the earnest prayer closes on the note of covenant renewal, our eyes are turned upward in anticipation of what God will do:

> Here we are, servants today!
> And the land that You gave to our fathers,
> To eat its fruit and its bounty,
> Here we are, servants in it!…
>
> And because of all this,
> We make a sure covenant and write it;
> Our leaders, our Levites, and our priests seal it.
> (Neh. 9:36, 38)

Did Ezra's generation really believe that they would act differently from the previous generations? Did they really think they would be covenant keepers? If they did, it wouldn't take them very long to realize they couldn't be faithful. They would again forsake the house of God, profane the Sabbath, marry pagan women, and defile the priesthood (Neh. 13:11, 17–18, 27, 29). What of God's covenant then? What person can keep the covenant?

Jesus came as the God-man, extending grace and mercy as the Lord of the covenant and fulfilling the covenant perfectly as the Servant of the covenant. What Israel continually failed to do, Jesus did. This prayer in Nehemiah is the gospel story. It reveals who God is (the covenant King and covenant keeper), who we are (covenant breakers), and points us forward to Jesus Christ, the humble Son of God and perfect Son of Man who lived a life of perfect obedience for us and died a cursed death in our place, taking the wrath of God on Himself.

Since Jesus has opened the throne room of grace to us again, let us not grow weary in prayer. It is a privilege that has been granted to us, and yet we often neglect it. We can confidently yet humbly come before our Father, recognizing His great name, repenting of our sins, requesting that our needs and desires be met, and rejoicing in the good gifts He has given to us.

* * * * *

It is not in the greatness of our prayers but in the greatness of the God to whom we pray that great things are accomplished. What is your view of prayer? Do you believe that God uses it as a means to accomplish His purposes and plans? Do you believe that prayer matters? The best answer to these questions comes from the amount of time you spend in prayer. And our greatest example is our Lord and Savior Jesus Christ, who withdrew from large crowds of people in order to gain strength, bolster His courage, enjoy unbroken communion, and receive His marching orders from His Father, an example we'll look at in the next chapter.

Time to Ponder and Pray

1. What questions have you had about prayer? Which ones have been answered by Scripture? Which ones remain unanswered? How would you answer someone who asked, "Do my prayers really matter?"

2. Spend time in confession, beginning with yourself and then moving on to your family, your local church, and then the universal church. How have you ignored the word of God? What specific sins have you committed this week?

3. Spend time humbling yourself before God's greatness as you recall the mighty acts that He has done in Scripture and during the last year of your life.

4. How are you being a witness in the places where God has put you? Ask God to give you the opportunity to be a light for Him.

5. Use Daniel's imperatives in your own prayer before God for your specific circumstances:

Hear…

Forgive…

Pay attention to…

Act…

Delay not…

For Your glory…

6. When was the last time you felt ashamed over sin before the holy God? How often do you identify yourself with the rebelliousness in your family and church, recognizing that all of life is covenantal?

7. In your prayers, how do you recognize who God is, who you are, God's words and works, and His power to act in behalf of His people?

8. In what ways do you grow weary in prayer? When are you most tempted to neglect praying? How have you been encouraged to persevere in prayer as you have read this chapter?

9. In light of what you've learned in this chapter, write out a prayer to God.

10. Seek to memorize Nehemiah 9:6.

8

The Lord Who Prays

The Inauguration of the Kingdom

One of the truths of the Christian faith that is most comforting to me is that Jesus is my High Priest. I have taught my children from the earliest age the truth that Jesus prays for them. I want them to know that He is interceding for them when they are tempted to sin. I need to grow in this awareness when I'm in the heat of tempta- tion. Instead, I often forget that Jesus is praying for me when I'm tempted not to love as I should, to find my joy and satisfaction in something other than Him, to not extend peace to my husband, to respond impatiently to my child, or to have an ungrateful heart when things aren't going my way. In those moments it's very comforting to remember that Christ is my High Priest. The Westminster Shorter Catechism 25 defines His priesthood like this: "Christ executeth the office of a priest, in his once offering up of himself a sacrifice to sat- isfy divine justice, and reconcile us to God, and in making continual intercession for us."

This truth comforts me for at least two reasons. First, I am deeply aware that I sin every day and fall far short of God's glory. To know that my Savior has satisfied God's justice for my sins and reconciled me to my heavenly Father is glorious news. Second, I know that Jesus is praying for me continually. He is not only in me by way of His Spirit, but He is for me. In other words, He doesn't want me to give in to the world, the flesh, and the devil. But when I do, which is often, He never says that I've crossed the line and there's no more grace for me. No, instead, He forgives me and continues to pray for me. As believers, we are to extend that same forgiveness and intercession to others. We forgive others because Christ has forgiven us. We pray for others because Christ prays for us. Digging deeper into Jesus's prayer life will encourage us in this endeavor, which is what this chapter is all about.

The Word Became Flesh

The Gospels record for us the amazing truth of the incarnation. Jesus came to earth and lived a life of perfect obedience, died for the sins of God's people, was raised as the firstfruits of the resurrection, and ascended to the Father.

It is only in Christ that the covenant King and the covenant servants meet. Christ is both the Lord and the Servant of the covenant. He has come as Lord to extend grace and mercy to God's rebellious servants, and He has come as the Servant of the covenant to perfectly fulfill what God's people could never fulfill, thus bringing blessing to all those who place their faith in Him.

Jesus came to do what no other prophet, priest, or king before Him had ever been able to accomplish. Because He humbled Himself and became obedient to death on the cross, God has highly exalted Him as Lord of all (Phil. 2:8–9). As Ed Clowney says, "He transforms prayer, because in him the communion with God which we seek in prayer becomes a reality. The psalmists sought the Lord in the temple; Simeon found him there."[1]

The Importance of Prayer in Jesus's Life

Jesus had many things to do during His earthly ministry. We might think that He would have put His relationship with His Father on hold while He did the work of redemption. Instead, communion with His Father was intricately connected with His work. The triune God is others-centered. Jesus did not leave communion with

---

1. Clowney, "Prayer," 694–95.

the Father behind in heaven when He came to earth. Instead, He sought His Father in prayer: "Now in the morning, having risen a long while before daylight, He went out and departed to a solitary place; and there He prayed" (Mark 1:35). Others were in a hurry for Him to preach, but Jesus put prayer before preaching (vv. 36–39). On another occasion, He gave thanks to the Father before feeding the five thousand (John 6:11), and afterward He dismissed the crowds and went up on the mountain by Himself to pray (Matt. 14:23). A rich prayer life does not happen haphazardly. It must be a priority and a habit. But once you know the sweet communion with the heavenly Father that prayer offers, it's a habit and priority you won't want to live without.

When Jesus had been baptized, He was praying, and the Holy Spirit descended on Him from heaven in bodily form like a dove. His Father spoke from heaven, saying, "You are My beloved Son; in You I am well pleased" (Luke 3:22). Great crowds gathered to hear Him speak and be healed of sicknesses, but Jesus would often withdraw to pray in desolate places (5:16). Before the dawning of the day when He chose His twelve apostles, He prayed on a mountain throughout the entire night (6:12–13).

Jesus wasn't always alone on the mountain praying. One time He took with Him Peter, John, and James. As He was praying, He was gloriously transfigured before them, and His Father spoke from heaven saying, "This is My beloved Son. Hear Him!" (Luke 9:35). When He raised Lazarus from the dead, He thanked His Father for hearing His prayer (John 11:41–42). And during the feast of Passover, in the midst of a crowd of people, He prayed,

> "Now My soul is troubled, and what shall I say? 'Father, save Me from this hour'? But for this purpose I came to this hour. Father, glorify your name."
>
> Then a voice came from heaven, saying, "I have both glorified it and will glorify it again." (12:27–28)

After Jesus's resurrection He appeared to two disciples on the road to Emmaus, and he ate a meal with them, blessing the bread before giving it to them (Luke 24:30). Before ascending to heaven,

He lifted up His hands and blessed His disciples (vv. 50–53). From start to finish, Jesus's ministry was filled with prayer. If our beloved Lord and Savior needed to pray, you and I need to pray all the more. Of course, Jesus's prayers were perfect. But by the power of His Spirit, prayer is transformed in our lives. By God's grace, we can learn to turn to God in prayer anytime, anywhere, about anything.

Jesus Teaches on Prayer

Jesus didn't just pray; He also taught others to pray. Jesus had been praying by Himself in a certain place, and after He had finished, one of His disciples said, "Lord, teach us to pray" (Luke 11:1). This is how it should be! Others should witness our prayer life and want to learn from us. A friend once asked if she could observe my devotional life so that she could grow in her personal prayer time and Bible study. Admittedly this was a bit awkward, but I told her that she could because I recognized her desire wasn't to critique me but to learn from me. How much greater to learn from Jesus Himself, who is perfect in prayer! So Jesus taught His disciples what has now become known as the Lord's Prayer (Luke 11:2–4; see also Matt. 6:9–13). This prayer that our beloved Lord and Savior taught His disciples teaches us many important aspects of prayer.

First, we pray to "our Father in heaven" (Luke 11:2) in order to "awaken in us…a childlike reverence and trust that through Christ God has become our Father, and [will not] refuse to give us what we ask in faith."[2] And we pray to our Father in heaven to focus our eyes on God's heavenly majesty and almighty power and to expect Him to supply all our needs.[3] Watching my husband be a father has been one of my greatest joys in life. How he delights to give our children their heart's desires! My own father was the same way. This is how it is with our heavenly Father. He loves to bless His children (vv. 11–13).

---

2. Heidelberg Catechism: 450th Edition, in *Comforting Hearts, Teaching Minds*, by Starr Meade (Phillipsburg, N.J.: P&R, 2013), Q. 120.

3. Heidelberg Catechism, Q. 121.

Second, we pray, "Hallowed be Your name" (Luke 11:2) in order to help us truly know God and honor, glorify, and praise Him for His works and His almighty power, wisdom, kindness, justice, mercy, and truth that shine forth from them. Also, this helps us direct our thoughts, words, and works in such a way that God's name will always be honored and praised.[4] Always honoring and praising God's name is hard to do, so we should pray it often! Our thoughts, words, and works are often directed to the honor and praise of our own name. Instead, we must honor and praise God's name as we go about our days; as we speak to our friends, family, and neighbors; and as we do the work the Lord has put before us.

Third, we pray, "Your kingdom come" (Luke 11:2) so that God will rule us by His word and Spirit in such a way that our submission increases, His church will grow, and the devil's work and all evil will be destroyed until God's kingdom is consummated.[5] You don't have to look very far to realize the extent of evil in this world. But there's coming a day when Jesus Christ will consummate His kingdom and there will be no more evil in the new heavens and new earth. Even now, as He rules believers with His word and Spirit, He is building His church and making us conform to Christlikeness.

Fourth, we pray, "Your will be done on earth as it is in heaven" (Luke 11:2), asking for help in rejecting our wills and accepting God's holy will and in faithfully and willingly carrying out the work He has for us.[6] It's so easy to be selfish! We want what we want when we want it. We grow weary of doing the good works the Lord has prepared for us to do. We must pray that we will be faithful and willing servants as we work for Christ. We must pray that we will say no to our flesh and yes to God's will.

Fifth, we ask, "Give us day by day our daily bread" (Luke 11:3). We desire God's care for our bodily needs so that we come to depend on Him alone for sustenance and recognize that no amount of worry

---

4. Heidelberg Catechism, Q. 122.
5. Heidelberg Catechism, Q. 123.
6. Heidelberg Catechism, Q. 124.

or work on the one hand, or God's gifts on the other, can do any good without God's blessing. It's a plea for us to stop trusting other things to meet our needs and to trust in God alone.[7] I don't know about you, but it's easy for me to trust in other things *plus* God. It's nice to have savings *plus* Christ. It's comforting to have employment *plus* the Lord. It's wonderful to have good friends who will help me when I ask *plus* Jesus. But to trust in God *alone* to meet my needs—that's hard. In fact, it's impossible apart from God's grace. But prayer changes us. As we come before Him with our needs, we will begin to rely on Him alone.

Sixth, we pray, "And forgive us our sins, for we also forgive everyone who is indebted to us" (Luke 11:4). We plead guilty and ask for Christ's blood to cover the sins we commit and the evil that constantly clings to us. We ask Him to forgive us in the same way that we, by God's grace in us, forgive those who sin against us.[8] The more we recognize our sin and need of a Savior and the more we stand in awe of His forgiveness for our sins, the more we will extend forgiveness to others. When we fail to forgive others who ask for our forgiveness, we're misunderstanding God's amazing grace in our own lives.

Finally, we cry, "And do not lead us into temptation, but deliver us from the evil one" (Luke 11:4). We acknowledge that we are too weak to fight the flesh, the world, and the devil, which constantly attack us, and we ask the Lord to strengthen and uphold us with the Holy Spirit's strength so that we are not defeated but are able to resist our enemies until Christ returns and we are finally glorified.[9] I use this as a prayer every morning. It's a stark reminder to me that I'm awakening to a battle. If my enemies never stop attacking me, then I never need to stop praying. I'm always in need of God's power to strengthen me, and it's never safe to let down my guard.

---

7. Heidelberg Catechism, Q. 125.
8. Heidelberg Catechism, Q. 126.
9. Heidelberg Catechism, Q. 127.

Jesus Prays for Peter

If there was anyone who was too weak to hold his own because of his sworn enemies and needed God's power to uphold him, it was Peter. Peter loved Jesus. He had seen Him transfigured on the mountain. He had defended Him in the garden of Gethsemane (Matt. 26:51–53). He had followed Him faithfully during His earthly ministry. But Peter was going to do something he never dreamed he would do, even when Jesus told him:

> Simon, Simon! Indeed, Satan has asked for you, that he may sift you as wheat. But I have prayed for you, that your faith should not fail....
>
> I tell you, Peter, the rooster shall not crow this day before you will deny three times that you know Me. (Luke 22:31–32, 34)

Sadly, Peter did deny Jesus three times: once before a servant girl in the courtyard of the high priest's house, then a little later before another man, and about an hour later before a different man. All three associated Peter with Jesus, and each time he denied he knew Him. As he was making his final denial, the rooster crowed, and the Lord looked at Peter. With that look from his Master and Savior, he remembered Jesus's words and went out and wept (Luke 22:54–62).

How could Peter deny Jesus, especially since Jesus was praying for him? He had prayed Peter's faith wouldn't fail, but it did—three times. What do we make of Jesus's prayer for Peter that seems to go unanswered? We have to turn to John 21 to understand how Jesus's prayer for Peter was answered. Unlike Judas, who betrayed Jesus and hung himself, Peter denied Jesus and wept over his unfaithfulness. After the resurrection, Jesus appeared to His disciples several times. The third time he met them for breakfast on the Sea of Tiberias. After they had finished breakfast, Jesus asked Peter three times (corresponding to his three denials), "Do you love Me?" Each time Peter told Jesus, "Yes, Lord; You know that I love You." After the third time his heart was grieved. Peter was sorry for his sin (John 21:15–17).

Peter's faith had not ultimately failed. The Lord had preserved his faith, even though he had denied his Savior three times on a dark night in Jerusalem. Jesus not only forgave Peter, but He commanded him to feed His sheep and to follow Him (John 21:15–19). What a beautiful testimony of God's grace and the efficacy of Christ's intercession for us! It is unlikely Peter thought Jesus's prayer would be answered in the way it was. But Jesus knew. Even as He prayed for Peter, He knew that Peter would deny Him. Indeed, He told Peter so. But He had also predicted that Peter would turn back to Him again. Apart from Christ's prayer, Peter would not have turned back to Christ. None of us would turn to Christ apart from His intercession. Our hearts are hard. We don't love Jesus without His intervention. But He prays for us, and because He prays, we are delivered from the Evil One.

Jesus Prays as Our Priest

Before the final events of His life that led up to His crucifixion, Jesus prayed what theologians call the High Priestly Prayer (John 17:1–26). This is Jesus's longest-recorded prayer in Scripture, and it teaches us several characteristics of prayer.

Jesus prayed for Himself: "Father, the hour has come. Glorify Your Son, that Your Son also may glorify You" (John 17:1). Through His death and resurrection, Jesus wanted His Father to glorify Him so that He could glorify His Father. Jesus had come to give eternal life to all whom the Father had given to Him. Jesus had glorified the Father on earth by accomplishing the work of redemption. Now He prayed that the Father would glorify Him: "And now, O Father, glorify Me together with Yourself, with the glory which I had with You before the world was" (v. 5).

Next, Jesus prayed for those the Father had given to Him: "I pray for them. I do not pray for the world but for those whom You have given Me, for they are Yours" (John 17:9). These disciples believed that the Father had sent His Son into the world; they heard the truth and received it. Jesus prayed for believers because upon His ascension to heaven they would remain in the world, and He knew the world was a hard place for believers to live. So He prayed, "Holy Father, keep through Your name those whom You have given Me, that they may be one as We are…[and] they may have My joy fulfilled in themselves" (vv. 11, 13). He prayed that the Father "should keep them from the evil one" (v. 15). And, "Sanctify them by Your truth. Your word is truth" (v. 17).

After praying for His disciples, Jesus prayed for future believers, those people who would come to saving faith through the testimony of believers. He prayed "that they all may be one, as You, Father, are in Me, and I in You; that they also may be one in Us, that the world may believe that You sent Me" (John 17:21). In other words, He prayed that their unity would reflect the unity He had with the Father, so that the world may believe the Father had sent the Son and loves His children as He loves His Son.

Finally, Jesus prayed for all believers, both present and future, to "behold My glory" (John 17:24). Because of His love for His Son from before creation, the Father gave His glory to Him, and Jesus desired that God's people would join Him in heaven and behold His glory. What a glorious day this will be! Right now, dear believer, whether you are battling hard against sin or crying out in the midst of suffering, be encouraged. One day we will behold our beloved Bridegroom's glory in the new heaven and new earth where there is no more sin and suffering. But even now, we are present with Christ through His Spirit, who indwells the hearts of believers.

Jesus closed by praying again for His disciples, "that the love with which You loved Me may be in them, and I in them" (John 17:26). This is the covenantal language of God's presence with His people that was used throughout the Old Testament, and now Jesus uses it in the Gospels. The consummation of this promise is found in the New Jerusalem (Revelation 21–22). Oh, how glorious that Jesus is with us! Throughout the Old Testament, God's presence had come to His people in the garden, in Moses's tent outside the camp, in the tabernacle, and then in the temple. Finally, Jesus came and tabernacled among God's people, full of grace and truth (John 1:14). His presence would never again leave His people. At His departure from this earth, He sent His Spirit to indwell His people so that He can continue to be in them until the day He will return and be with them forever.

Jesus's prayers should inform our prayers. We should pray that we would be one with our brothers and sisters in Christ. We should pray for the Lord to keep our loved ones and church family from the Evil One. We should ask God to sanctify us and our brothers and sisters in Christ in the truth. We should plead with the Lord to use our witness to lead others to saving faith. And we should ask the Lord to display the love of Christ in and through our lives in our marriages and families, careers, ministries, and friendships.

Prayer on the Mount of Olives

After Jesus had shared the Passover meal with His disciples, He went to the Mount of Olives, as was His custom. This was the place where He retreated to rest and spend refreshing time with His Father. This was the mountain from which He had come down to enter Jerusalem (Luke 19:29) and on which he lodged each night between His days of teaching in the temple (21:37). The disciples followed Him. When He came to "a place called Gethsemane" (Matt. 26:36), He told His disciples to pray that they may not enter into temptation (Luke 22:40; see also 11:4).

Jesus went a short distance away from His disciples to pray His own prayer: "Father, if it is Your will, take this cup away from Me; nevertheless not My will, but Yours, be done" (Luke 22:42). The "cup" was the cup of God's wrath and judgment against all of the sins of His people. Since God is just, someone had to pay for His people's sins. And that someone had to be perfect in order to stand in our place. There was only One who could do that, Jesus. He alone was both God and man, the perfect God-man, who could atone for our sins on Calvary. But in His human state, it was far from easy. On the cross, His Father's back was turned against Him, and His Father's wrath was poured out on Him. His agony was so great during His prayer in Gethsemane that "His sweat became like great drops of blood falling down to the ground" (v. 44).

Sadly, while the disciples were supposed to be praying, they fell asleep. Jesus, knowing what He was about to endure and having just poured out His soul in agony to His Father, questioned why they were sleeping and simply repeated His instructions, "Rise and pray, lest you enter into temptation" (Luke 22:46). We need to do this too. Often we move through life as if we are sleeping, with eyes closed toward spiritual things. Our Lord reminds us that we must not fail to pray that we will follow God's will and not be tempted to follow the ways of the world, the flesh, or the devil.

Prayer from the Cross

Jesus was not the only man led away to Golgotha to be crucified, but He was the only innocent man. Two criminals were led away with Him; one would be hung on a cross on Jesus's right side and the other on His left. The first thing that Luke records Jesus saying on the cross is, "Father, forgive them, for they do not know what they do" (Luke 23:34). This recalls Isaiah 53:12:

> Therefore I will divide Him a portion with the great,
> And He shall divide the spoil with the strong,
> Because He poured out His soul unto death,
> And He was numbered with the transgressors,
> And He bore the sin of many,
> *And made intercession for the transgressors.*

As Jesus hung on the cross He cried out, "My God, My God, why have You forsaken Me?" (Matt. 27:46). This was in fulfillment of Psalm 22:1. Since the book of Psalms doesn't include stories that advance the narrative of redemption, I haven't looked at the prayers recorded there in this book. But because the book of Psalms is filled with prayers, I want to consider this psalm in its original context and then how Jesus fulfills it.

Psalm 22 reminds us that there is no suffering as great as separation from God:

> My God, My God, why have You forsaken Me?
> Why are You so far from helping Me,
> And from the words of My groaning?
> O My God, I cry in the daytime, but You do not hear. (vv. 1–2)

This is exactly what hell will be like. Those who want nothing to do with God will be granted their desire for eternity. But David, the author of this psalm, was not an unbeliever. He had a relationship with God, and so feeling separated from Him seemed unbearable. But instead of turning toward inner turmoil, he turned toward truth and trusted God:

> But You are holy....
>
> Our fathers trusted in You;
> They trusted, and You delivered them.
> They cried to You, and were delivered;
> They trusted in You, and were not ashamed. (vv. 3–5)

In David's ongoing struggle with his circumstances, he was honest before the Lord. He recognized his enemies as the ferocious beasts they were, "strong bulls" (v. 12), "a raging and roaring lion" (v. 13), and "dogs" (v. 16). But he recognized more his eternal Creator, who had made him trust Him from birth: "You are He who took Me out of the womb; You made Me trust while on My mother's breasts" (v. 9). Though he felt as though death would swallow him, he knew the One who could swallow death and placed his confidence in Him, declaring, "You have answered Me" (v. 21).

Psalm 22 also teaches that suffering in faith ends in singing: "I will declare Your name to My brethren; in the midst of the assembly I will praise You" (v. 22). The lone sufferer doesn't remain alone. He moves into the covenant community, declaring the name of the Lord to his brothers, praising Him and calling others to praise Him too. David stood in the midst of them as a witness to God's faithfulness, leading them in worship, "You who fear the LORD, praise Him!" (v. 23). The King of all the earth has a host of worshipers gathered about Him. Not just the Jews or even the Gentiles but also those who are not yet born will praise Him because our redemption has been secured: "They will come and declare His righteousness to a people who will be born, that He has done this" (v. 31).

It is Jesus who tells His Father's name to His brothers, praising Him in the midst of the congregation, leading God's people to worship Him (Heb. 2:11–13). He has saved both Jews and Gentiles by making one new man through the cross. Kingship belongs to the Lord Jesus Christ, who has been given the nations as His inheritance. Forsaken by the Father as He hung on the cross, He has accomplished our redemption. Yes, He has done it; it is finished.

What are we to do with such glorious news? We are to receive it by faith. Then we are to respond in thanksgiving by worshiping God, working for His glory, and witnessing to the nations about Him. Our suffering should not end with silence but with singing in the midst of the covenant community. This is the very heart of prayer. We don't suffer alone. God is with us. We can talk to Him anytime, anywhere, about anything. God's people are also with us. We should ask them to pray for us. One day our petitions-plus-praise will turn to praise alone as we sing the song of the Lamb in the new heaven and new earth.

Before Jesus took His final breath He said, "Father, into Your hands I commit My spirit," (Luke 23:46). This fulfilled Psalm 31:5: "Into Your hand I commit my spirit; You have redeemed me, O LORD God of truth." This statement reveals why Jesus did what He did and how He did it. We read His prayer in the garden of Gethsemane in Luke 22:42: "Father, if it is Your will, take this cup away from Me; nevertheless not My will, but Yours, be done." Jesus was fully submitted to His Father's will, and in His last dying breath He displayed that by committing His spirit to Him. This is how all of us endure through suffering, by submitting our will to the Father's will and by committing our very lives to Him.

* * * * *

Do you find yourself encouraged by the truth that Jesus is your High Priest, interceding for you on a daily basis? Are you teaching this to your children and grandchildren and to those you minister to in your church, workplace, and neighborhood? You, dear reader, need Jesus praying for you. Your sin is great, but His grace is greater. Your temptations are also great, but Jesus is praying that you will not fall.

As we grow in our awareness that Christ prays for us, we will grow in praying for others, something we will look at more fully in the next chapter.

Time to Ponder and Pray

1. How does knowing that Jesus is your High Priest, who satisfied God's justice and intercedes for you, motivate you to pray?

2. How do you view your prayer life? Does prayer happen haphazardly, or is it a priority and a habit? How have prayer times in the past given you a desire to have more of them?

3. What obstacles get in your way of turning to God in prayer anytime, anywhere, about anything?

4. What did you learn about the Lord's Prayer that challenged you? Convicted you? Comforted you?

5. How does Jesus's prayer for Peter encourage you? Which person do you need to pray for who is battling a particular temptation? Spend time in prayer for him or her now.

6. Which of these area(s) do you need to pray about: for unity with other believers, deliverance from the Evil One, sanctification in the truth, effective evangelism, or the love of Christ to abound in your life? Be specific about your need.

7. Spend time in prayer today for yourself, your family, and your church family—that you will not enter into temptation, that you will submit to the Father's plans, and that you will grow in your prayer life.

8. In what way(s) are you suffering? Has your suffering led to silence or singing, and why? Why is praise the very heart of prayer?

9. In light of what you've learned in this chapter, write out a prayer to God.

10. Seek to memorize Matthew 6:9–13.

The Lord Who Is with Us by His Spirit

The Interadvent Age

One of the greatest gifts we can give to our brothers and sisters in Christ is prayer. When we ask fellow believers how we can pray for them intentionally and follow through consistently, that's a gift. Over the years, I have come to delight in asking people how I can pray for them and then doing it—regularly and methodically. As I come before the throne of grace, their names are on my lips, asking God to answer the requests they've shared with me. This knits my heart together with theirs. My love for them grows. I'm invested in their ministries, their singleness, their marriages, and their families. And I want the best for them. This takes time and work, but Scripture doesn't suggest we pray; it commands us to pray.

Prayer is a privilege. When we consider that Christ has reconciled us to God the Father through the cross so that we can pray (as well as other things), it changes how we view prayer. Duty turns to delight. Praying for others brings us closer to God. Through prayer we draw near to our Father and talk with Him. Wow! Our great God wants to hear from us. He cares about our family and friends. He wants to turn His ear to us. He delights to extend grace and mercy. He is never too busy, otherwise occupied, in a bad mood, or too tired or uninterested. When He hears our voice, we have His attention. We can intercede for our fellow believers, asking God to grant them grace and mercy to repent of their sin, persevere in their suffering, and bear the fruit of righteousness that comes through Christ. In this chapter we will see how precious and profound it is when believers pray for other believers.

The Promise of the Holy Spirit

After His resurrection Jesus appeared to His disciples over a forty-day period, speaking about the kingdom of God. He commanded them not to depart from Jerusalem but to wait for the promise of the Father, the baptism of the Holy Spirit. He told them that they would be His witnesses, beginning in Jerusalem and in all Judea and Samaria and to the ends of the earth. Then He was lifted up in a cloud into heaven from Mount Olivet (Acts 1:1–11). When His apostles returned to Jerusalem, they went to the upper room where they were staying. The apostles, with the women and Jesus's mother, Mary, and Jesus's siblings, devoted themselves to prayer (vv. 12–14). One of the matters for prayer was who would replace Judas as an apostle. Two men were under consideration, but which should they choose? They prayed, acknowledging the Lord knows the hearts of all, and asked Him to show them which one He had chosen to take Judas's place (v. 24). Then they cast lots. The lot fell on Matthias, the Lord's choice, so he became the twelfth apostle, replacing Judas.

When they were all together on the day of Pentecost, the Holy Spirit came upon them, just as Jesus had promised (John 16:4–15; Acts 1:5, 8). This was an important event in the history of redemption signifying that the new covenant age had arrived. It's not that the Holy Spirit had been inactive before Pentecost because the Spirit of God was active in the creation of the world (Gen. 1:2), but now His presence was more powerful and personal. His more powerful presence was displayed on the day of Pentecost when three thousand souls were added to the church. His personal presence is displayed in Romans 8:

> For as many as are led by the Spirit of God, these are sons of God. For you did not receive the spirit of bondage again to fear, but you received the Spirit of adoption by whom we cry out, "Abba! Father." The Spirit Himself bears witness with our spirit that we are children of God....

The Spirit also helps in our weaknesses. For we do not know what we should pray for as we ought, but the Spirit Himself makes intercession for us with groanings which cannot be uttered. Now He who searches the hearts knows what the mind of the Spirit is, because He makes intercession for the saints according to the will of God. (vv. 14–16, 26–27)

The New Testament reveals that we pray to the triune God; we pray to the Father through the Son by the power of the Holy Spirit.

A Prayer for Boldness

Peter and John had been arrested for healing a crippled man (see Acts 3:2–9; 4:1–3). After the rulers decided to release the apostles, the first place they went was to the covenant community. They knew how important community was for their growth in Christ and in ministry. The believers were their *friends* (4:23 ESV). I hope you can say that about your church—that it is a place where you have made friends and the first place you go when you are in trouble. But more importantly, I hope that you can say your church is a place of prayer. The first thing these believers did when they learned that Peter and John were in trouble was to pray *together* (v. 24). They recognized the importance of corporate prayer.

This reminds us of King Hezekiah and his people, who were also in trouble and went to the Lord in prayer: "O LORD of hosts, God of Israel, the One who dwells between the cherubim, You are God, You alone, of all the kingdoms of the earth. You have made heaven and earth" (Isa. 37:16). These believers also began their prayer by recognizing who God is. He is the one true God who created all things (Acts 4:24). He is also the covenant God who speaks to His covenant people through the mouth of His chosen instruments (v. 25). Their prayer was filled with the Old Testament Scriptures, reflecting both the Psalms (see Ps. 146:6) and the Prophets (see Jer. 4:10; Dan. 9:8). But they also directly quoted Scripture. Acts 4:25–26 quotes Psalm 2:1–2:

Why do the nations rage,
And the people plot a vain thing?
The kings of the earth set themselves,
And the rulers take counsel together,
Against the Lord and against His Anointed.

In its original context, the psalm encouraged the king of Israel and the people, who were being attacked by their enemies. The Lord had made a covenant with David that he would have a descendant on his throne forever, and the psalm reminded the people of the nations' futility to try to overthrow God's decree. During times of such attack, they could find safety in the Lord's sovereignty. But even Israel recognized that the Anointed in the psalm must have been referring to someone greater than an earthly king; they believed this spoke of the Messiah to come. By the time of the New Testament, it was clear that the Anointed was Jesus Christ.

After much adoration, the believers made their request in Acts 4:29: "Now, Lord, look on their threats, and grant to Your servants that with all boldness they may speak Your word." They had already spoken boldly before their opponents (see v. 13); now they prayed that they would continue to do so. They finished the prayer by acknowledging that it is the sovereign Lord who heals and performs signs and wonders through the name of His holy Servant Jesus (see Isa. 52:13).

God responded to the believers' prayer in three ways (Acts 4:31). The place in which they were gathered was shaken (see also 2:1–3). Then they were all filled with the Holy Spirit. Finally, they continued to speak the word of God with boldness, which was in direct answer to their petition (v. 29). We can be sure that the Lord will answer our requests when we pray according to His will.

Perhaps prayer is one of the most abandoned activities in our churches today. This is detrimental. With all of his business and duties, Martin Luther recognized the vital necessity of prayer if any of his duties were to be accomplished. Rather than tack on prayer as another duty, it was the first appointment of his day—one that lasted three hours![1] He realized that prayer was not just another duty, but the foundation for accomplishing all the duties in his day.

Our own sin, ignorance, and physical weakness, as well as Satan's constant attempts to thwart us, are all the more reasons to take Ephesians 6:18 to heart: "praying always with all prayer and supplication in the Spirit, being watchful to this end with all perseverance and supplication for all the saints." We must stand firm in the battle by praying. As that great man of prayer E. M. Bounds reminds us, "[Great leaders of the Bible] were not leaders because of brilliancy of thought, because they were exhaustless resources, because of their magnificent culture or native endowment, but because, by the power of prayer, they could command the power of God."[2]

The Power of Prayer

In the book of Acts we learn about a woman named Tabitha, or Dorcas, who had suffered greatly with an illness from which she died. Tabitha was a disciple of the Lord, "full of good works and charitable deeds" (Acts 9:36). But lying physically dead in an upper room did not allow her to be an active part of the church anymore. And this caused much grief to all the widows who had spent their time with her, benefiting from her ministry.

But the disciples in Joppa were not grieving without hope. They had likely heard of Jesus raising Lazarus from the dead (John 11:1–44) and restoring life to the widow's son in Nain (Luke 7:11–15) and to the ruler's daughter (Matt. 9:18–25). So they sent for the apostle Peter. While the widows were busy showing Peter the good works Tabitha had done, he was concerned with the work the Lord had called him to do. He put everyone outside the room and knelt down to pray, knowing that he was just an instrument in desperate need of the Lord's power.

---

1. J. Oswald Sanders, *Spiritual Leadership* (Chicago: Moody Press, 1994), 86.
2. E. M. Bounds, *Prayer and Praying Men* (London: Hodder & Stoughton, 1921), as quoted in Sanders, *Spiritual Leadership*, 92.

By faith Peter believed in the power of the Lord and turned to the body, saying, "Tabitha, arise" (Acts 9:40). Jesus's words at the house of the ruler of the synagogue must have been echoing in Peter's heart and mind: "Talitha cumi," which means, "Little girl, I say to you, arise" (Mark 5:41). Like the disciples at Joppa, Peter may have also recalled other times the Lord had raised the dead to life, Elijah raising the widow's son (1 Kings 17:17–24), and Elisha raising the Shunammite's son (2 Kings 4:18–37).

How overwhelmed with joy the saints must have been when Peter presented Tabitha alive to them! The miracle that occurred in Joppa reminds us that the kingdom of God has already come. It was a signpost, pointing forward to the day when our bodies will be raised to new life, glorified to live in the new heaven and the new earth, at the consummation of the kingdom. In the meantime, we're reminded of the importance of prayer as we minister to others in the name of Jesus. When the Lord calls us to do a work for Him, no matter how great or small, we must start on our knees.

The Effectiveness of Prayer

King Herod was harassing believers and killed James the brother of John and put Peter in prison, "but constant prayer was offered to God for him by the church" (Acts 12:5). That night an angel of the Lord woke up Peter and led him out of the prison. Once he realized he was free, Peter didn't waste any time. He went to share with his prayer warriors how their prayers had been answered. He didn't have to guess where to find them. They were meeting at the house of Mary, John Mark's mother (v. 12). Many had gathered there to earnestly pray for Peter. Luke, the author of Acts, wants us to know how important prayer is and that it should stand behind every decision we make, every task we perform, and every ministry in which we engage. Here he wants us to see that the prayers of the saints were effective, moving prison guards and a prison gate.

Moving quickly through the dark streets in the middle of the night, Peter was not on a leisurely visit. When he knocked at the door of Mary's gate, he must have been in a great hurry to get off the dangerous streets, where he could easily be seen. But that is not exactly what happened. When Rhoda, one of the servant girls, recognized Peter's voice, she was so full of joy that she forgot to open the gate! Instead, she ran to tell the praying believers that Peter was at the gate. But just as the women who told the apostles that Jesus was risen were met by men who thought they were telling an idle tale (Luke 24:10–11), Rhoda was met with disbelief and an accusation: "You are beside yourself!" (Acts 12:15). Thankfully, Rhoda was persistent. She believed what she had heard, even if the others didn't. The believers concluded that Rhoda had seen Peter's angel, but she persisted, and Peter kept knocking. Finally, they opened the door, saw that it was really Peter, and were amazed.

You can only imagine the whooping and hollering they wanted to do! But Peter motioned for them to be silent. He had news to tell! He wanted to boast of how the Lord had brought him out of prison, and he gave all glory to God for what He had done. The church's earnest prayers for Peter had been effective.

Prayer in Prison in Philippi

Peter wasn't the only one who experienced imprisonment. In Acts 16:25–40 we learn that Paul and Silas had been accused before the magistrates for their words and works in Philippi. They had been beaten with rods and thrown into prison, and their feet had been fastened in stocks. But instead of writhing in pain and desperation, they were praying and singing hymns to God!

While Paul and Silas were praying and singing hymns to God in prison, other prisoners were listening to them. In the midst of pain and persecution, they were proclaiming the gospel with their prayers. This was evangelism at its finest hour. As Paul and Silas were shaking the foundations of heaven with their praying and singing, heaven was shaking the foundations of the prison with an earthquake, opening the doors and unfastening everyone's bonds. Again, the sovereign Lord displayed His power in answer to the prayers of His people.

We should pray and sing hymns often both when we're alone and when others can hear us. We never know who is listening. Our children see us on our knees and hear us sing praises to the Lord. Often they will do the same. My oldest daughter used to sing hymns and read the Bible to her baby dolls, which transitioned from the world of play to the real world as she cared for her younger siblings or little ones in the church nursery.

Luke makes clear that prayer was an important part of Paul's ministry (Acts 20:36; 21:5; 22:17; 28:8), but this becomes even clearer when we study Paul's prayers in his letters to various churches. We will consider several.

A Praise Report

Paul's mission in life was to make sure his disciples were standing strong in the Lord, so the encouragement Timothy brought him regarding the Thessalonian church led to thanksgiving (1 Thess. 3:6–10). The hearts of Paul, Silvanus, and Timothy swelled with joy before God the Father, and they continued to constantly pray that He would give them the opportunity to teach the believers in Thessalonica more about the faith. How a word of encouragement breathes life into our weary souls! When the Lord blesses us with the opportunity to know about the steadfast faith of other disciples, it should lead us to give thanks for the work of sanctification He is accomplishing in their lives.

Paul's thanksgiving fueled his petitions (1 Thess. 3:11–13). He prayed to "our God and Father" and "our Lord Jesus Christ" to "direct [their] way" to the Thessalonian believers (v. 11). He desire the Lord to "make [the Thessalonians to] increase and abound in love to one another and to all" just as their love was increasing and abounding for the Thessalonians (v. 12). He prayed for the Lord to sanctify them, to "establish [their] hearts blameless in holiness before our God and Father" (v. 13). In his prayer, he recognized that the Thessalonian believers' present life was intricately connected with the future coming of Christ with His saints (v. 13). The prophet Zechariah also tied holiness with the coming day of the Lord: "In that day 'HOLINESS

TO THE LORD' shall be engraved on the bells of the horses" (Zech. 14:20). The Lord saves His people from sin in order to sanctify them.

Paul's prayer is a model for us today. We should cry out to our heavenly Father often. When we feel Satan is hindering us in ministry, we should ask God to direct our steps in fruitful ways. As we disciple others, we should pray that the Lord makes their love for Him and others grow. We must also recognize it's the Lord who sanctifies those believers with whom we're tempted to become short-tempered or impatient. We must keep our focus on the coming of Christ and strive for holiness together as we depend on God's grace to live for His glory.

Praise to God for the Thessalonians

In 2 Thessalonians 1:3–10 Paul recognizes God's grace at work in the Thessalonian church and praises God for several things. He begins by thanking God because their "faith grows exceedingly" (v. 3). The Thessalonian believers aren't just taking baby steps toward a robust faith; they are growing by leaps and bounds. This is cause for great thanksgiving! Paul also thanks God because "the love of every one of [them] all abounds toward each other" (v. 3). This is not natural. Left to ourselves we are selfish, but God's grace and peace are at work in the Thessalonian church in a mighty way, and the people's love for each other is growing. Paul and his team even boasted about the Thessalonians to the other churches they came into contact with "for [their] patience and faith in all [their] persecutions and tribulations that [they] endure" (v. 4). If there's ever a time when faith and love wane, it's during persecution and affliction. We question God's presence, protection, and promises. We doubt His love for us. We forget about the grace and peace He has extended to us, and we fail to extend it to others. But Paul goes to the heart of prayer, praising God for His grace in the Thessalonians' lives.

Steady Prayers for the Thessalonians

Paul's prayers for the Thessalonians were not sporadic but steady. To Paul, the churches he planted were his children (1 Thess. 2:7). They were never out of his heart and thoughts. He continually prayed for them. In 2 Thessalonians 1:11–12 he asked God to make them worthy of His calling. In other words, Paul prayed for their sanctification. God calls us out of darkness and sin into the light and purity of His Son. We are freed from sin to be holy. We aren't first worthy of God's calling and then called by Him. We are called by God and then made worthy of His calling by the grace of God. Paul also requested that God would fulfill every resolve for good and every work of faith by His power. Paul recognized that resolutions and work were nothing apart from God's power. If the Thessalonians were going to glorify God and be glorified in Him, it would have to come by His grace and power.

So it is with you and me. We cannot make ourselves worthy of God's calling. God calls us while we are still sinners and then gives us the grace and power to walk in a manner worthy of Christ. Likewise, we can't resolve to be good on our own. We need the power of God to bring our resolution to fruition. And we can't work for the Lord without His power. A life worthy of His calling is rooted in His grace and power. This is a good prayer for both our physical and church families: *Father, grant us Your grace and power to walk worthy of Your calling.*

A Thanksgiving Prayer for the Ephesians

Paul's thanksgiving prayer for the saints in Ephesus (Eph. 1:15–23) is grounded in the spiritual blessings believers have in Christ (vv. 3–14). But Paul is particularly thankful for their "faith in the Lord Jesus" and their "love for all the saints" (v. 15). Their love shows no particularity. God calls us to love all our brothers and sisters in Christ, even the ones we may find difficult to love. What Paul heard with his ears (their faith and love) filled his heart with thanksgiving, so that his lips did "not cease to give thanks for [them]" (v. 16). What a beautiful reminder that as we hear of our brothers' and sisters' faith and love, we should engage in heartfelt prayer for them.

Paul lifts his readers' eyes to "the God of our Lord Jesus Christ, the Father of glory" (Eph. 1:17), for indeed what the Father has done through Christ is glorious. And all glory dwells in the Godhead. Paul asks the Father to give the Ephesian believers a deep, rich, thorough knowledge of Him—not knowledge about Him, but a beautiful relationship in which they truly and intimately know Him. The Holy Spirit working in believers is the only way they can have a spirit of wisdom and revelation, which in turn gives them (and us) spiritual eyesight to know more accurately and to more deeply appreciate all the spiritual blessings they have in Christ.

Paul wants believers to have greater eyesight with regard to "the hope of His calling" (Eph. 1:18). Romans 8:28–30 states, "And we know that all things work together for good to those who love God, to those who are called according to His purpose. For whom He foreknew, He also predestined to be conformed to the image of His Son, that He might be the firstborn among many brethren. Moreover whom He predestined, these He also called; whom He called, these He also justified; and whom He justified, these He also glorified." This passage helps us understand that our hope is rooted in the past, when God called us to be His children. It is active in the present, as we enjoy the benefits of justification, adoption, and sanctification. And it is fixed on the future, in which we have hope that we will one day be like Him and reign with Him for all eternity.

Paul also wants believers to have sharper eyesight concerning "the riches of the glory of His inheritance in the saints" (Eph. 1:18). Think about the truth that believers are God's rich and glorious inheritance! God chose us to be His treasured possession (Ex. 19:6; 1 Peter 2:9–10). When we grasp this truth, it will make our heart sing! And such knowledge certainly whets our appetite to know God more. In a culture that longs for a secure identity, we certainly have one to offer. God's people are His treasure.

Furthermore, Paul prays believers will have better eyesight in relation to the "exceeding greatness of His power toward us who believe" (Eph. 1:19). God's power is so great that it can't be measured. It is specifically for believers, not for the world in general. And it's according to the "working of His mighty power" (v. 19). In other words, God has greatly and mightily worked power in Christ, and that same power is available for the lives of believers. This power is everything we need to live the life God has called us to as His treasured possession. It is the power we cling to when sin threatens to undo us. It is the power we recognize when suffering knocks on our door. And it is the power that upholds us when our service for God is so far beyond our capability we're tempted to give up. That kind of power changes everything!

In order to help his readers grasp how deep and how wide the power of God is, Paul gives the illustration of Christ's resurrection and ascension, "which He [God the Father] worked in Christ when He raised Him from the dead and seated Him at His right hand in the heavenly places" (Eph. 1:20). The same power God worked in Christ to raise Him from the dead and exalt Him in glory is the same power He gives to His children. Paul alludes to Psalm 110:1, the most-quoted Old Testament verse in the New Testament, in Ephesians 1:20. God the Father says to God the Son, "Sit at My right hand, till I make Your enemies Your footstool." The power at work among the persons of the Godhead is the same power at work among saints that make up the church. This is incredible news!

But Paul goes on. He wants to emphasize, particularly in a culture in which Roman emperors are deified, that Christ is "far above all principality and power and might and dominion, and every name that is named, not only in this age but also in that which is to come" (Eph. 1:21). Paul relies on another psalm for this point: "You have made him to have dominion over the works of Your hands; You have put all things under his feet" (8:6). In the context of the psalm, David is writing about the dominion humankind has received from God. To be sure, it was marred by the fall, but the cultural mandate still remained in effect. But Paul's point here is that Christ, as the second Adam, is the ultimate fulfillment of this psalm: "He put all things under His feet" (Eph. 1:22). God the Father has given to Christ dominion over the works of His hands and has put all things under His feet.

The Father has given this Christ, who is Lord over all, to the church, "which is His body, the fullness of Him who fills all in all"

(Eph. 1:22–23), so that He, as its head, might fill it with His fullness, which is already filling the entire universe. That should transform our thinking about the church! The church is the means through which the Father will showcase His power to a watching world in order that He might be glorified, the gospel might be proclaimed, and the world might be transformed. This means all our work done in the name of Jesus Christ and for the building up of the church is in line with God's eternal purposes. How often do you pray that your church family will be used to showcase God's power to a watching world?

A Prayer for Inner Strength

Prayer is an immense privilege and a means of grace we should not neglect. Through prayer we come to know something of the enormous love God has for us. We also learn what it means to offer our hearts to Christ for His home.

In Ephesians 3:14–21 we read another of Paul's prayers for the church in Ephesus, which he loved. He begins with "the Father of our Lord Jesus Christ, from whom the whole family in heaven and earth is named" (vv. 14–15). He is not praying to the Father of only the Jews or only the Gentiles, but to the Father of all the redeemed, regardless of whether they are Jew or Gentile, male or female, slave or free. The Father of the redeemed both in heaven (the church triumphant) and on earth (the church militant) is the Father of fathers who gives us status as children of God. This is the Father we bow before because of "Christ Jesus our Lord, in whom we have boldness and access with confidence through faith in Him" (vv. 11–12).

Such truth should bring us to our knees in prayer. Our hearts should be warmed to the triune God. Our lips should be moved to petition and praise, our ears open to hear the word of God and to use it in prayer, and our hands raised in adoration of our Father, Savior, and Comforter. Paul's prayer is instructive as he pleads before the throne of grace.

Paul's main request is that the believers will be "strengthened with might through [the Holy] Spirit in the inner man" (Eph. 3:16).

His request is bold because of the riches of God's glory, which he has already written about in his letter (see 1:3–14, 18; 2:4–7; 3:8), and because of the Spirit's power. He wants Christ to dwell in their hearts by faith. It's not that Christ doesn't dwell in their hearts. He certainly does, or Paul wouldn't have been able to speak of the riches these believers have in Him (see, for example, 1:3–14). But Paul wants his readers to understand that there's a difference between us welcoming Christ as a visitor to our hearts and asking Him to take up permanent residence as the owner and manager of our hearts. In other words, he wants us to be controlled by Christ, specifically by the love of Christ. In fact, he emphatically states that we are rooted and grounded in Christ's love (3:17).

These two images come from different lines of work—agricultural and architectural. Christ's love is the soil in which love for Him and love for others grow. And Christ's love is the foundation on which love for Him and love for others are built. It cannot be the other way around. "We love Him because He first loved us" (1 John 4:19). But we need strength to comprehend Christ's love.

Paul is at a loss to describe what is immeasurable, yet he resorts to using terms of measurement, "width and length and depth and height" (Eph. 3:18). We need God's strength and God's saints to comprehend it, and even then we will comprehend it truly, but not fully; for all of eternity we will continue learning more and more of Christ's love for us. What is Paul's greatest hope in praying for the believers to be strengthened in their inner being? That they "may be filled with all the fullness of God" (v. 19). In other words, that they will be Christlike.

Paul's prayer climaxes in a doxology, or declaration of praise, for God's goodness and glory: "Now to Him who is able to do exceedingly abundantly above all that we ask or think, according to the power that works in us, to Him be glory in the church by Christ Jesus to all generations, forever and ever. Amen" (Eph. 3:20–21). Paul is careful to build a strong case for God's power. God is able. He is able to do. He is able to do far more. He is able to do far more abundantly. He is able to do far more abundantly than all that we ask. He is able to do far more abundantly than all that we think. And all this is "according to the power that works in us" (v. 20). The same power that raised Jesus Christ from the dead is at work in us (Eph. 1:19–20). We have resurrection power! From one generation to another and from one age to the next, God will receive praise in Christ and His church as His manifold wisdom is displayed to all.

The more overwhelmed we are with the love our great God has for us, the more overcome we will be to get on our knees in prayer and the more eager we will be to let Christ take up residence in our hearts as the administrator of our affections and the master of our motives. This in turn will lead to a life of prayer and praise in which we often see God's power at work within us and in our brothers and sisters in order to display His glory through Christ and the church from generation to generation and from age to age. Let it be so!

Praise to God for the Philippians

As a mom, I am grateful for the thanksgiving I receive from my children. I love to serve them, and I would serve them meals and attend to their needs regardless of whether they thanked me, but it is a delight to hear them say, "Thank you, Mom." It's no different for our heavenly Father when we talk to Him. He delights to hear our thanksgiving. Thanksgiving is one of the ways we praise God when we pray. Paul had learned the joy of thanking God, and in his prayer for the Philippians (Phil. 1:3–11), it's instructive that Paul doesn't begin with a list of material blessings, but with the people God has put in his life. He thanks God for the memories he has made with the Philippians.

Every time Paul prayed for the Philippians, he began by thanking God for them: "I thank my God upon every remembrance of you" (Phil. 1:3). Surely this included gratitude for material blessings too, such as the gift they sent him in Thessalonica to meet his needs (4:14–18). But it wasn't that the Philippians gave just monetary gifts; Paul was thankful for their "fellowship in the gospel from the first day until now" (1:5)—from the time he had planted the church in Philippi until the present—including all they did to help further the gospel message in their spheres of influence. This fellowship in the gospel filled him with great joy.

It's also instructive that Paul was thankful for *all* of the Philippian believers. He didn't have favorites. If it seems challenging to you to love and thank God for every believer in your congregation, notice that Paul's affection was rooted in his certainty that God would sanctify each of His children and preserve them until Christ's return: "Being confident of this very thing, that He who has begun a good work in you will complete it until the day of Jesus Christ" (Phil. 1:6).

Since Paul recognized that the Philippians were "partakers with [him] of grace" (Phil. 1:7), he was confident of their salvation and sanctification and loved them with the affection of Christ Jesus. Since the Philippians couldn't see Paul's heart of affection, he called on God as his witness, the only One who knows our hearts completely and rightly (Jer. 17:9–10), to convey to them how "greatly I long for you all with the affection of Jesus Christ" (Phil. 1:8), an affection based in his union with Christ and in his communion with the saints in Philippi. Can you honestly say that you yearn for every member of your church family with the affection of Jesus Christ? And does this affectionate yearning lead you to pray for them?

Paul's main prayer for the Philippian church is that their "love may abound still more and more" (Phil. 1:9). In his letter to the Corinthians, he wrote that love is greater than both faith and hope (1 Cor. 13:13). This is because when Christ comes again our faith will be sight and our hope will be realized, but our love for our beloved Savior and for each other will go on for all eternity. Paul's prayer for the Philippians to have abounding love is a reflection of Christ's command: "A new commandment I give to you, that you love one another; as I have loved you, that you also love one another. By this all will know that you are My disciples, if you have love for one another" (John 13:34–35). Jesus's words, of course, weren't new. They were rooted in God's law: "You shall love the LORD your God with all your heart, with all your soul, and with all your strength" (Deut. 6:5); and "You shall love your neighbor as yourself " (Lev. 19:18).

Paul's definition of *love* has substance. It's not the kind of love we might read about in a Valentine's Day card or sing about in a love song. It is knowledgeable and discerning love. He prays "that your love may abound still more and more in knowledge and all discernment" (Phil. 1:9). It is bound by the knowledge of God's holy will and spiritual wisdom and understanding that come from above (Col. 1:9; James 3:17–18). Such knowledgeable and discerning love is not an end in itself, but the means to an end. It gives us the ability to approve what is excellent, which means we'll be pure and blameless as the bride of Christ on the day our Bridegroom returns. It also means that we'll be filled with the fruit of righteousness that comes through Christ. Such abounding love and righteous fruit will glorify God. It is His gracious work from start to finish, and He will receive the praise for it.

The imagery of the fruit of righteousness has its roots in the Old Testament. In fact, it serves as an introduction to the entire book of Psalms. In Psalm 1 the psalmist depicts a contrast between the righteous and the rebellious that becomes a thread running throughout the entire book. The righteous man is said to be "like a tree planted by the rivers of water, that brings forth its fruit in its season" (Ps. 1:3; see also Prov. 11:30; Jer. 17:7–8). Jesus uses this imagery in John 15:1–5, teaching His disciples that only those who abide in Him will bear much fruit. The fruit of righteousness is possible only by the Spirit of God, not by our own willpower (Gal. 5:22–23). And it doesn't come easily. The Father disciplines us in order to produce the fruit of righteousness in our lives to His own glory and praise (Heb. 12:11).

* * * * *

Are you ready to give the gift of prayer to those around you? Make a commitment to ask others how you can pray for them, and follow through consistently. Take their names before the throne of grace. Your love for them will grow, and you'll be invested in their lives, wanting the best for them. Yes, it takes time and work, but Scripture exhorts us to pray. It's a means of grace God has given to us. Your heavenly Father wants to hear from you. He cares about your family and friends. When He hears your voice, you have His attention. He is ready to extend grace and mercy. Don't delay; talk to Him today.

Time to Ponder and Pray

1. Describe a time when you offered to pray for someone regularly. What did it mean to that person? How did it change your relationship for the better?

2. How does your church show that it prioritizes prayer in all of its ministries? In what ways is there room for growth in this area, and how could you help?

3. In whose company do you need to pray and sing hymns to God, asking God to use this to bring him or her to either a saving or deeper faith?

4. In whose life do you see God's grace at work as he or she remains steadfast in the faith in the midst of trials? Spend time praising God for what He is doing in his or her life.

5. Pray that God will give the pastors and elders of your church His grace and power to walk worthy of His calling (2 Thess. 1:11–12).

6. Pray that those in your church will recognize the value of their work done in Jesus's name so that they will eagerly serve, knowing they are doing work of eternal significance.

7. How should our understanding of God's love impact our prayer life?

8. Why is it important that your prayers be filled with thanksgiving alongside petitions, and how do you show gratitude in your prayers?

9. In light of what you've learned in this chapter, write out a prayer to God.

10. Seek to memorize Philippians 1:9–11.

10

The Lord Who Is Coming Soon

The Consummation of the Kingdom

Have you ever wondered what prayer will be like in the new heaven and the new earth? No longer will you pray for the Lord to take away the pain you're experiencing from a broken heart or body. No longer will you ask God to deliver a loved one from death. No longer will you mourn over the injustice you face. No longer will you ask God to comfort your child as she cries over not having friends at school. No longer will you pray for the Lord to deliver you from the Evil One, freeing you from the temptation of immorality or idolatry. No longer will you ask God to protect you and your loved ones from murderers and liars and sexual assault. There will be no more prayers for prodigal children or cancer treatments, hurting marriages or infertility, injuries or illnesses, unemployment or financial distress. No longer will you cry out for deliverance from anger and depression, addiction and disillusionment. No longer will you ask the Lord to act justly and righteously or help you to understand and trust His ways. No longer will you plead with the Lord to help your unbelief or bolster your hope. There will be no more prayers for racial reconciliation, the eradication of abortion, an end to sex trafficking, and a decrease in high school dropouts. No longer will we pray for the Lord to humble and save ungodly leaders or to bring mercy to our country in the wake of serious sin.

For what will we pray then? We have already learned that praise is the heart of prayer, so it shouldn't surprise us that in heaven praise will take center stage. "No longer will there be anything accursed, but the throne of God and of the Lamb will be in it, *and his servants will worship him.* They will see his face, and his name will be on their foreheads. And night will be no more. They will need no light of lamp or sun, for the Lord God will be their light, and they will reign forever and ever" (Rev. 22:3–5 ESV).

The New Heaven and the New Earth

There is coming a day when our beloved Lord and Savior, Jesus Christ, will descend in a cloud from heaven to claim His bride and usher her in to the new heaven and the new earth. At that time He will judge the living and the dead. The unrighteous will be cast into hell, and the righteous will inhabit the New Jerusalem. God's kingdom, which was inaugurated with Christ's life, death, resurrection, and ascension, will finally be consummated.

As Paul says in his letter to the Corinthians,

> For as in Adam all die, even so in Christ all shall be made alive. But each one in his own order: Christ the firstfruits, afterward those who are Christ's at His coming. Then comes the end, when He delivers the kingdom to God the Father, when He puts an end to all rule and all authority and power. For He must reign till He has put all enemies under His feet. The last enemy that will be destroyed is death. For "He has put all things under His feet." But when He says, "all things are put under Him," it is evident that He who put all things under Him is excepted. Now when all things are made subject to Him, then the Son Himself will also be subject to Him who put all things under Him, that God may be all in all. (1 Cor. 15:22–28)

During the Old Testament era, God's people went to the tent of meeting, tabernacle, or temple to pray, but in the New Jerusalem, "the Lord God Almighty and the Lamb are its temple. The city had no need of the sun or of the moon to shine in it, for the glory of God illuminated it. The Lamb is its light" (Rev. 21:22–23). The covenant promise will be consummately fulfilled: "Behold, the tabernacle of

God is with men, and He will dwell with them, and they shall be His people. God Himself will be with them and be their God" (v. 3).

This is not a return to Eden. This is far superior to the garden in which the Lord God placed Adam and Eve. In Eden Adam and Eve could sin, but they didn't have to sin. If they had obeyed, they would have been confirmed in their righteousness. Tragically, they sinned, and all humankind fell with them in that first transgression. But in the New Jerusalem, believers won't be able to sin. The New Jerusalem is more expansive, more excellent, and more extensive than Eden, filled with multitudes of people from every tribe, tongue, and nation worshiping God in glorified bodies.

Worship in the New Jerusalem

We must turn to the last book of the Bible, Revelation, to get a taste of what worship will be like in the New Jerusalem. Throughout the book of Revelation, the apostle John records different songs. We can begin to sing these songs even now, for the author of Hebrews says, "You have come to Mount Zion and to the city of the living God, the heavenly Jerusalem, to an innumerable company of angels, to the general assembly and church of the firstborn who are registered in heaven, to God the Judge of all, to the spirits of just men made perfect, to Jesus the Mediator of the new covenant, and to the blood of sprinkling that speaks better things than that of Abel" (12:22–24). Because Christ has already come, we have already come to Mount Zion. The kingdom choir has already been inaugurated. But because Jesus has not yet come again, we are not yet the consummated kingdom choir. Worship in the New Jerusalem will be infinitely more glorious than our worship is now. No longer will there be sin or suffering impeding our worship. We will be completely sanctified, free from sin and suffering. We will sing like we've never sung before!

Praise for God's Holiness and Sovereignty

In the new heaven and the new earth, we will praise God for His holiness and sovereignty. He alone is sovereign over creation and worthy of the glory, honor, and praise for such a mighty work that is sustained by Him alone (Rev. 4:9–11). Isaiah had learned this: "I saw the Lord sitting on a throne, high and lifted up" (Isa. 6:1). Daniel had also learned this: "The man clothed in linen...held up his right hand and his left hand to heaven, and swore by Him who lives forever" (Dan. 12:7). In contrast to earthly kings who are only temporal, God is the "King of heaven, all of whose works are truth, and His ways justice" (Dan. 4:37).

I wonder how many bored and sleepy people would be in our worship services if they grasped that we have already come to the heavenly Jerusalem. Since our most incredible worship experiences on earth are only a glimpse of what they one day will be, we should be filled with hope and joy as we wait for that day. Our worship of Christ here on earth is one of the most dynamic tools of witness that we have. As our neighbors watch us leave our homes every Sunday for worship, maybe they will wonder at this God whom we serve and perhaps their hearts will be softened by the Spirit so that they might join in worshiping Him.

Praise for God's Worthiness

Believers will spend an eternity praising God for His worthiness. In Revelation 5:9–10 we learn a "new song" that the saints sing. In the Old Testament this new song is associated with praise for God's creation, righteousness, salvation, and justice (Pss. 33:3–6; 96:1; 98:1; 149:1); victory over destruction (Ps. 40:1–3); and victory in war (Ps. 144:9–10). In Revelation the new song is associated with Christ's redemption, which began with His death, resurrection, and ascension and will be consummated at His second coming. This too was anticipated in the Old Testament (see Ex. 12:1–28; Isa. 53:7; Dan. 7:10, 22–27; 12:9).

The angels join in worshiping Christ for His work of redemption, ascribing to Him seven attributes, again conveying His complete worthiness of worship (Rev. 5:11–12). He receives worship for His "power and riches and wisdom, and strength and honor and glory and blessing!" (v. 12; see also 1 Chron. 29:11–12; Dan. 2:20; 7:10).

The creatures and the elders also fall down in worship (Rev. 5:13–14; see also Dan. 7:13–27). The creatures ascribe to the Lamb four attributes, again conveying His complete worthiness of worship. He is worthy of "blessing and honor and glory and power" (Rev. 5:13) for all eternity. Both the Father and the Son are worshiped by all creatures everywhere, pointing to the consummation, during which "every knee should bow, of those in heaven, and of those on earth, and of those under the earth, and that every tongue should confess that Jesus Christ is Lord, to the glory of God the Father" (Phil. 2:10–11). Today is still the day of salvation. Let us pray for our unbelieving family, friends, neighbors, fellow students, and coworkers, asking God to save them.

Praise for God's Salvation

In the new heaven and new earth, we will praise God for His work of salvation. In Revelation 7:9 we read of "a great multitude which no one could number, of all nations, tribes, peoples, and tongues" worshiping God (vv. 10–12). This scene of worship is already taking place in part with the saints who have gone before us, but it will not be fully consummated until after the final judgment, when the new heaven and new earth will be full of all God's people.

We see in these verses the fulfillment of the promise to Abraham in Genesis 13:16: "And I will make your descendants as the dust of the earth; so that if a man could number the dust of the earth, then your descendants also could be numbered." This offspring is made up of both Jews and Gentiles, all those who by faith are part of the people of God. This is a picture of the culmination of God's covenantal story of redemption and restoration that was prophesied in the Abrahamic covenant.

The people of God are "standing before the throne and before the Lamb, clothed with white robes, with palm branches in their hands" (Rev. 7:9). These white robes are Christ's white robes of righteousness and the palm branches signify His victory over the war with the world, the flesh, and Satan. These palm branches recall the Festival of Tabernacles, an annual thanksgiving Israel celebrated to remember

God's deliverance at the Red Sea and His protection and provision as they "tabernacled" in tents during their wilderness journey from Egypt to the Promised Land (Lev. 23:40, 43). This feast has now been completely fulfilled in Christ.

Believers praise God the Father and God the Son for the work of redemption, "Salvation belongs to our God who sits on the throne, and to the Lamb!" (Rev. 7:10). God the Father sent His Son into the world to redeem His people. God the Son, in perfect obedience, accomplished the work of redemption. And God the Holy Spirit applies the work of redemption to us.

All the angels stood around the throne and the elders and the four living creatures, and fell on their faces before the throne and worshiped God (see Rev. 5:11–12). The elements of their worship instruct us how to praise God. Blessing comes to us from God, and we are to bless God. Glory is to be given to Him alone for the plan of judgment and salvation. God's plans and purposes are wise. Our lives are to be a continual act of thanksgiving before God, to whom all honor is due. And it is because of His power and might that redemption has been made possible for the redeemed.

Praise for God's Kingship

Believers will worship God for His kingship in the new heaven and new earth. In Revelation 11:16–17 we read of twenty-four elders (heavenly representatives of the church) "who sat before God on their thrones [and] fell on their faces and worshiped God" (v. 16). This is the appropriate posture of worship. Whether we are literally facedown or facedown in the posture of our hearts, we are to humble ourselves before the almighty God who has accomplished His kingdom purposes. The elders gave thanks to Him:

> We give You thanks, O Lord God Almighty,
> The One who is and who was and who is to come,
> Because You have taken Your great power and reigned. (v. 17)

This is something that we do not do often enough on this side of glory but will continually do in the New Jerusalem. Even now, instead of grumbling and complaining, we can, by God's grace, give thanks to the Lord for who He is and for all that He has done for us. He is the Lord God Almighty who is and who was. In the consummated kingdom, Christ reigns over all for eternity by His great power that overcame the darkness.

We often overlook this aspect of God's sovereignty in our prayer life. Too often we offer our pleas before God and then attempt to fix problems on our own, make happen the situation that we want, or overcome sin by our own strength. But God is sovereign over the details of our lives and is the only one who has the power to accomplish His purposes for them. We must plead with Him and put our trust in Him.

Praise for God's Righteous Acts

For all of eternity believers will praise God for His righteous acts. In Revelation 15:3–4 the saints who have experienced the second exodus sing the "song of Moses, the servant of God, and the song of the Lamb." Moses's song, sung after the first exodus (Exodus 15; Deuteronomy 32), is called the song of the Lamb because Moses, the servant of God, anticipated the Servant of servants, Jesus Christ. This song of the Lamb both celebrates the redemption of God's people and pronounces judgment over God's enemies.

The song acknowledges that God's works are "great and marvelous" (Rev. 15:3; see also Ex. 34:10; Ps. 111:2–4) and that He is "Lord God Almighty" (Rev. 15:3). His works display His justice and truth, and His saints affirm, "just and true are Your ways" (v. 3; see also Pss. 11:7; 33:5; 97:2). He was never a God confined to Israel but was always "King of the nations" (v. 3 ESV; see also Ps. 2:7–9). As King over the nations, He alone has the ability to use the nations to accomplish His purposes and plans for His people. So both God's character and conduct are worshiped.

There is no one who will not fear and glorify His name, for at the end of the age, "every knee should bow…and…every tongue should confess that Jesus Christ is Lord, to the glory of God the Father" (Phil. 2:9–11). His righteous acts will have finally been revealed in all of their fullness: "And there were loud voices in heaven, saying, 'The kingdoms of this world have become the kingdoms of our Lord and of His Christ, and He shall reign forever and ever!'" (Rev. 11:15). His holiness, both His moral purity and the sum of all His divine attributes, will be worshiped. And all nations will be represented before His throne (Pss. 86:9–10; 98:2; Jer. 10:7).

Look at the deeds God has done in your life. Count them, meditate on them, tell your family about them, and praise God for them. Recognize His sovereignty over the events in your life. There is no chance or luck, and there are no mistakes. God has orchestrated the events of your life for His purposes. His ways are just and true. We can trust Him when we cannot trust ourselves. We can trust His way when we cannot see our way through the darkness. We can trust that He rules over all of the circumstances and relationships in our lives and is using them for our good. Praise God!

Praise for God's Love

The climactic song in the book of Revelation, as well as in Scripture, is found in Revelation 19:6–7: "Alleluia! For the Lord God Omnipotent reigns! Let us be glad and rejoice and give Him glory, for the marriage of the Lamb has come, and His wife has made herself ready." The consummation of His kingdom has displayed that He is almighty and that He reigns (see also Ps. 47:8; Isa. 52:7; Ezek. 1:24). The church rejoices and exults and gives God glory. The marriage of the Lamb has come (see also Isa. 61:10; Hos. 2:14–20; 2 Cor. 11:2; Eph. 5:25)! By the power of the Holy Spirit, the church has withstood the world system, with its fires of persecution, deception, and temptation, and she is ready. She stood firm as a witness and as a worshiper, proving that she was worthy to marry the Lamb. Without the refining fires of persecution, deception, and temptation, she never would have been ready to marry the Bridegroom. But God used these things to make her ready for His Son and granted her clothes of fine linen, clean and bright.

While we are clothed with fine linen, clean and bright, at the marriage of the Lamb at the end of history, even now we are clothed with pure linen by the Holy Spirit of God so that we may stand alongside our Lord and Savior, Jesus Christ, and have access to the throne of grace (Heb. 4:16). The relationship that we now have with the triune God is an intimate one. Because of Christ's righteousness, we can sing to our heavenly Father unashamed and unhindered. But let us never forget that He sang over us first:

> The LORD your God in your midst,
> The Mighty One, will save;
> He will rejoice over you with gladness,
> He will quiet you with His love,
> He will rejoice over you with singing. (Zeph. 3:17)

* * * * *

What prayers are you praying that you will be glad to leave behind when Jesus returns? Perhaps you're weary of asking Him to take away your pain or the injustice you face. Maybe you're tired of praying for the Lord to deliver you from the Evil One, freeing you from the temptation of immorality or idolatry. Perhaps you are ready to no longer pray about cancer treatments, hurting marriages or infertility, injuries or illnesses, unemployment or financial distress. One day our prayers will completely give way to praise: "No longer will there be anything accursed, but the throne of God and of the Lamb will be in [the Holy City], and his servants will worship him. They will see his face, and his name will be on their foreheads. And night will be no more. They will need no light of lamp or sun, for the Lord God will be their light, and they will reign forever and ever" (Rev. 22:3–5 ESV).

Time to Ponder and Pray

1. How have you imagined prayer in the new heaven and the new earth? How has this chapter informed your thinking in new and different ways?

2. Before you read this chapter, did you realize that believers are already part of the kingdom praise choir that was inaugurated at Christ's death and resurrection? What are your thoughts as you consider this truth?

3. In what ways could your prayer and praise be your greatest gospel witness to those around you?

4. Who do you need to pray for today to bow his or her knee in worship of the true God?

5. How do you show that your life is a continual act of thanksgiving before God, to whom all honor is due?

6. Describe a time when you have offered your pleas before God and then attempted to fix a problem on your own, make a situation happen that you wanted, or overcome sin by your own strength. Spend time in prayer confessing this to the Lord, and then pray that you will trust Him with your pleas.

7. How often do you count the deeds God has done in your life, meditate on them, tell your family about them, and praise God for them? Begin doing so today. Consider making a list in a journal that you can add to as the weeks and months go by.

8. Write a poem or compose a song about God's love. You may want to sing one of your favorite hymns about God's love to get you started. If you don't have a favorite, consider "And Can It Be" by Charles Wesley or "How Deep the Father's Love for Us" by Stuart Townend.

9. In light of what you've learned in this chapter, write out a prayer to God.

10. Seek to memorize Revelation 4:11.

Bibliography

Beale, G. K. *The Temple and the Church's Mission: A Biblical Theology of the Dwelling Place of God*. New Studies in Biblical Theology. Downers Grove, Ill.: IVP Academic, 2004.

Clowney, E. P. "Prayer." In *New Dictionary of Biblical Theology*, edited by T. Desmond Alexander, Brian S. Rosner, D. A. Carson, and Graeme Goldsworthy, 691–96. Downers Grove, Ill.: IVP Academic, 2000.

Dempster, Stephen G. *Dominion and Dynasty: A Theology of the Hebrew Bible*. New Studies in Biblical Theology. Downers Grove, Ill.: IVP Academic, 2003.

Hamilton, James M. *What Is Biblical Theology? A Guide to the Bible's Story, Symbolism, and Patterns*. Wheaton, Ill.: Crossway, 2014.

Heidelberg Catechism: 450th Anniversary Edition. In *Comforting Hearts, Teaching Minds* by Starr Meade. Phillipsburg, N.J.: P&R, 2013.

Ivill, Sarah. *The Covenantal Life: Appreciating the Beauty of Theology and Community*. Grand Rapids: Reformation Heritage Books, 2018.

Johnson, Dennis E. *Him We Proclaim: Preaching Christ from All the Scriptures*. Phillipsburg, N.J.: P&R, 2007.

Lillback, Peter A., ed. *Seeing Christ in All of Scripture: Hermeneutics at Westminster Theological Seminary.* Philadelphia, Pa.: Westminster Seminary Press, 2016.

Marshall, I. Howard, A. R. Millard, J. I. Packer, and D. J. Wiseman, eds. *New Bible Dictionary.* 3rd ed. Downers Grove, Ill.: IVP Academic, 1996.

Rosner, B. S. "Biblical Theology." In *New Dictionary of Biblical Theology,* edited by T. Desmond Alexander, Brian S. Rosner, D. A. Carson, and Graeme Goldsworthy, 3–11. Downers Grove, Ill.: IVP Academic, 2000.

Vos, Geerhardus. *Biblical Theology: Old and New Testaments.* 1975. Reprint, Edinburgh: Banner of Truth, 2007.

Walton, John H., Victor H. Matthews, and Mark W. Chavalas. *The IVP Bible Background Commentary: Old Testament.* Downers Grove, Ill.: IVP Academic, 2000.

The Westminster Confession of Faith and Catechisms. Lawrenceville, Ga.: Christian Education and Publications, 2007.

Scripture Index